HOW TO SURVIVE AN
ATOMIC ATTACK

EDITED BY JOHN CHRISTOPHER

AMBERLEY

Above: Schoolchildren practicing the 'Duck and Cover' drill, sheltering under the furniture when the sirens announce a nuclear attack. *(US Library of Congress)*

First published 2014.

Amberley Publishing
The Hill, Stroud, Gloucestershire, GL5 4EP
www.amberley-books.com

British Library Cataloguing in Publication Data.
A catalogue record for this book is available from the British Library.

ISBN 978 1 4456 3997 0 (print)
ISBN 978 1 4456 4008 2 (ebook)

Typesetting by Amberley Publishing.
Printed in Great Britain.

INTRODUCTION TO A MAD WORLD

On 29 August 1949, the Soviet Union detonated its first nuclear device. This event plunged the world into a new era, one in which the opposing nations of the East and West confronted each other across an ideological divide knowing that both sides had the capacity to destroy the other, and possibly the entire human race. This was the Cold War, a period of aggressive posturing which has no defined start point, although the Berlin Blockade of 1948–49 and the beginning of the Korean War in 1950 will suffice. The next decade saw a rapid build-up of high-yield atomic weapons in the belief that a full scale nuclear exchange could only be averted if neither side had any expectation of survival. Beginning in 1955, the US Strategic Command (SAC) kept one-third of its bomber force on alert, ready to take-off at fifteen minutes' notice to strike against Soviet targets. By the 1960s the SAC had upped the ante and part of its fleet of B-52 bombers remained in the air at all times, and by then both sides had the newly-developed Inter-Continental Ballistic Missiles (ICBMs) on permanent readiness. The US strategist John von Neumann is credited with the acronym that sums up this balance of destructive capability. MAD – Mutually Assured Destruction.

As with any conflict, cold or hot, the propagandists were at work engendering public support for the government's actions. In no small part this was achieved

Below: Schematic of the National Defense Pattern, from *Survivial Under Nuclear Attack*, published in 1950.

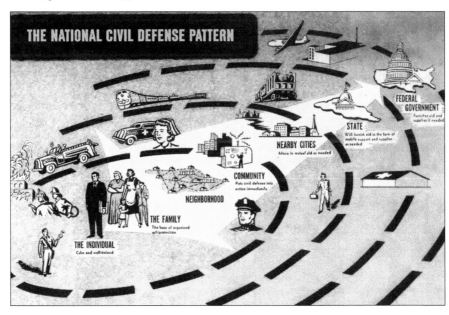

by whipping up the civilian population into a state of heightened anxiety. It is not by chance that this was the classic period for science fiction movies depicting alien invasions. In *The Day the Earth Stood Still* a flying saucer puts down in front of the White House. The analogy was obvious. But it was also the role of a government to protect its citizens as best it can and in the USA a National Civil Defense programme was instigated, and, as the diagram overleaf shows, right at its epicentre was the individual and family. When the bombs came, Joe Public had to fend for himself. Fortunately, self-help was at hand through the pages of a number of official booklets, and three of these form the basis of this compilation. In order of inclusion they are:

Fallout Protection – What to Know and Do About Nuclear Attack (1961)
Family Shelter Designs (1962)
Survival Under Atomic Attack (1950)

Viewed from the perspective of fifty or more years, it is hard to appreciate the impact that the contents of these matter-of-fact booklets muct have had on ordinary people. Apart from providing information on the nature of a nuclear attack – with a handy 'Words to Know' section explaining terms such as A-Bomb and H-Bomb, Kiloton, Megaton, Ground Zero and the various types of fallout – the emphasis was on practical steps to protect themselves. As President John F. Kennedy stated in a speech in July 1961, 'In the event of attack, the lives of those families which are not hit in the nuclear blast and fire can still be saved if they can be warned to take shelter and if shelter is available. We owe that kind of insurance to our families and to our country.' So while their children were being taught to 'Duck and Cover' at school, their parents constructed backyard shelters of plywood sheeting and concrete blocks, covered by soil or sandbags.

These documents on how to survive an atomic attack, with their illustrations of typical American families preparing for Armageddon, are at once surreal in their Pop Art style and absolutely chilling.

FALLOUT PROTECTION

WHAT TO KNOW AND DO ABOUT NUCLEAR ATTACK

EPARTMENT OF DEFENSE • OFFICE OF CIVIL DEFENSE

CONCERNING THIS BOOKLET

One of the first tasks assigned to me by the President, after I assumed responsibility for the Federal Civil Defense Program last August, was to give the American people the facts they need to know about the dangers of a thermonuclear attack and what they can do to protect themselves. This booklet attempts to provide the facts.

The factual information in this booklet has been verified by independent scientific authority, and represents the best consensus of the scientific community that we can establish.

The booklet also describes the national civil defense program. This program necessarily rests on judgments about what are prudent precautions in the light of our knowledge of what might happen and our evaluation of scientific facts. Judgments may differ. It is my considered judgment that this is a reasonable and prudent program—and that it is the best program we can have, measured against the other priorities of our national life.

Robert S. McNamara

Secretary of Defense

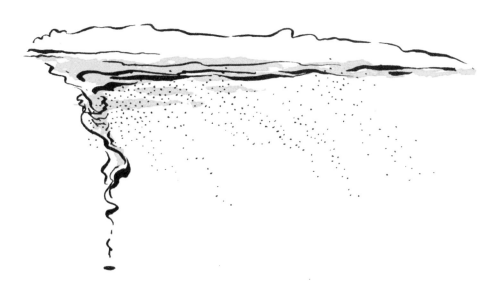

WHAT YOU SHOULD KNOW
AND WHAT YOU SHOULD DO

How to survive attack and live
for your country's recovery

The purpose of this booklet is to help save lives if a nuclear attack should ever come to America. The foreign and defense policies of your Government make such an attack highly unlikely, and to keep it unlikely is their most important aim. It is for this reason that we have devoted so large an effort to creating and maintaining our deterrent forces. However, should a nuclear attack ever occur, certain preparations could mean the difference between life and death for you.

The need for preparation—for civil defense—is likely to be with us for a long time, and we must suppress the temptation to reach out hastily for short-term solutions. There is no panacea for protection from nuclear attack. In a major attack upon our country, millions of people would be killed. There appears to be no practical program that would avoid large-scale loss of life. But an effective program of civil defense could save the lives of millions who would not otherwise survive. Fallout shelters and related preparations, for example, could greatly reduce the number of casualties.

President Kennedy, speaking on July 25, 1961, put it this way: "In the event of attack, the lives of those families which are not hit in the nuclear blast and fire can still be saved if they can be warned to take shelter and if that shelter is available. We owe that kind of insurance to our families and to our country."

The President was talking about shelter from radioactive fallout. The blast, heat, and fire of a nuclear explosion are appallingly destructive. But radioactive fallout could spread over thousands of square miles, covering a much greater area than the area endangered by fire and blast. Fallout would be a potential killer of millions of unprotected persons, but it also is a hazard that individuals and communities can prepare for through reasonable programs and actions. A fallout shelter program is one of these. This booklet contains information about a shelter program—what the Federal Government intends to do, and how State and local governments, and individual citizens can work together to bring it into being as a sound measure of national preparedness.

There is much we can do together, and perhaps the first step is to take a clear look at nuclear warfare and what it could mean to the world as we know it today.

There is no escaping the fact that nuclear conflict would leave a tragic world. The areas of blast and fire would be scenes of havoc, devastation, and death. For the part of the country outside the immediate range of the explosions, it would be a time of extraordinary hardship—both for the Nation and for the individual. The effects of fallout radiation would be present in areas not decontaminated. Transportation and communication would be disrupted. The Nation would be prey to strange rumors and fears. But if effective precautions have been taken in advance, it need not be a time of despair.

These are somber subjects, and they presuppose a catastrophe which can be made very unlikely by wise and positive policies, pursued with imagination and faith. Still, realistic preparation for what might happen is far more useful than blindness, whether from fear or ignorance. A sane and sober person can assume that, whatever comes to pass, he would draw on his reserve of courage and intelligence—and the unquenchable will to live—and begin to build again.

The experience would be terrible beyond imagination and description. But there is much that can be done to assure that it would not mean the end of the life of our Nation.

There are no total answers, no easy answers, no cheap answers to the question of protection from nuclear attack. But there *are* answers. Some of them are in this booklet.

WORDS TO KNOW

A-BOMB AND H-BOMB. Popular terms for what should correctly be called nuclear weapons. An atomic or A-bomb explodes through the fission (splitting) of atomic nuclei; a hydrogen or H-bomb is called a thermonuclear weapon because tremendous heat is needed to start the fusion process.

KILOTON. The power of nuclear weapons is measured in equivalents of the explosive energy of TNT. A one-kiloton weapon has the explosive equivalent of 1,000 tons of TNT.

MEGATON. The explosive equivalent of one million tons of TNT. In this booklet, a five megaton nuclear weapon exploded at or near ground level is assumed as a basis for describing explosive effects. There are much larger weapons which could do more damage, but the damage from larger weapons does not increase in direct ratio to the size of the weapons.

GROUND ZERO. The surface point at or above which a nuclear weapon detonates.

FIREBALL. The large, swiftly expanding sphere of hot gases, producing brilliant light and intense heat, that is the first manifestation of a nuclear explosion. After about a minute, the fireball fades into the atmosphere.

BLAST (SHOCK) WAVE. The near-solid wall of air pressure produced by a nuclear explosion. Beginning at more than 2,000 miles per hour, its speed decreases rapidly with distance.

BLAST WIND. The wind gust which travels with the blast wave and may be of many times hurricane force.

ROENTGEN. A unit for measuring an amount of radiation exposure.

INITIAL (PROMPT) RADIATION. The burst of gamma rays and neutrons sent out from the explosion during the first minute after detonation. Initial radiation is most deadly within about two miles of ground zero.

FALLOUT. The radioactive debris of a nuclear explosion, which eventually falls to earth in particles. The amount of fallout is enormously greater if a weapon detonates on or near the surface than if it explodes high in the air. Large amounts of earth are drawn up by the fireball. High in the sky, radio-active elements are incorporated into the earth particles, which are scattered by winds and in time fall to the ground.

FALLOUT RADIATION. The radiation emitted by fallout particles. Each particle of fallout gives off radiation as though it were a miniature X-ray machine. This radiation consists chiefly of beta rays (dangerous only if fallout particles touch the skin or are swallowed or inhaled) and gamma rays. Gamma rays, like X-rays, are very penetrating, and create the need for protective shields (fallout shelters).

EARLY FALLOUT. The fallout that returns to earth during the first day. This booklet is mainly about early fallout. The radioactivity of such fallout decreases rather rapidly at first, and more slowly as time passes.

SOME BASIC FACTS

The probable effects of nuclear attack and the relative value of certain protective measures are complex subjects. There is no attempt here to discuss them in great detail, but to present information that might be helpful in understanding the overall problem.

Effects of a 5-megaton burst

A five-megaton nuclear burst at ground level would destroy most buildings two miles from the point of the explosion. Steel-frame buildings would be knocked sideways and great fires started.

The destruction five miles away would be less severe, but fires and early fallout could be a significant hazard.

At 10 miles, sturdy buildings would remain intact. At this distance fires probably would not be started by the fireball, but might be started by the blast wave which could rupture gas lines and short-circuit wires. Flying glass would present a major danger, as would early fallout.

At 50 miles from the bomb burst, all buildings would remain standing. The fading blast wave would take about five minutes to arrive, but would still shatter many windows. The greatest danger at this distance would be from early fallout which would begin arriving in some areas within three or four hours, depending upon weather conditions at the time.

Danger of fire storms

When nuclear or incendiary bombs strike a highly combustible city area, they can create a "fire storm"; the rising column of hot gases draws in surrounding cool air, producing inward-blowing winds that confine the fire storm to the blast damage area. Primary fires would be a much greater hazard than fire storms. For maximum fire damage, a nuclear weapon must be detonated high in the air. This would eliminate most of the potential fallout hazard. The spread of fires from a nuclear attack would be limited in the same ways as are peacetime fires—by barriers such as open space, rivers, highways, by rainfall, and by varied distribution of burnable material.

Exposure to radiation

During the average lifetime, every human being receives about 10 roentgens of nuclear radiation from natural sources. In addition, people are exposed to small amounts of radiation in dental and chest X-rays and even from the luminous dials of wrist watches.

When large amounts of radiation are absorbed by the body in short periods of time, sickness and death may result. In general, the effects of radiation stay with people and accumulate over a period of time. Few people get sick who have been exposed to 100 roentgens or less. Exposure to more than 300 roentgens over a period of a few days will cause sickness in the form of nausea, and may cause death. And death is certain if a person receives an exposure of 1,000 roentgens over a period of a few days.

Young people might be injured more by nuclear radiation than older people. This is because young people are more apt to absorb radioactive elements into their bones and internal organs than are older people. Since young people are potential parents, they should be protected as much as possible following a nuclear attack to minimize the possible genetic effects on their descendants resulting from too much exposure to nuclear radiation.

Radiation sickness not contagious

Radiation sickness is neither contagious nor infectious. Fallout radiation cannot make anything radioactive. Food and water that have been exposed to fallout radiation are contaminated only to the extent that they contain fallout *particles*. Exposed food that may have particles on it can be made safe by washing, brushing, or peeling. Fallout particles can be removed from water supplies by sedimentation or filtering. People who have fallout particles on their bodies or clothing probably would not carry enough to endanger other people, but they should wash themselves for their own protection.

Long-term effects of radiation

Following a nuclear attack, most radioactive elements in fallout would decay rapidly, losing most of their power to harm. However, for some time thereafter the hazard could continue to restrict normal activities in some parts of the country. A few elements, such as strontium 90, cesium 137, and carbon 14, are long-lived and could harm humans in some ways, such as by being absorbed by food plants. However, the long-term damaging effects of such exposure are not yet known in great detail.

Radiation in the air

Following a nuclear attack the air would be contaminated by radioactive fallout only to the extent that it *contained fallout particles.* The most dangerous fallout particles—early fallout—would reach the earth in the first day after the detonation, but their mere passage through the air would not contaminate the air. Fallout particles in harmful amounts would not be present in basement family shelters. People in underground family shelters could keep fallout particles out of their shelters by having a simple hood over the air-intake pipe. Special filters are not needed for small shelters. However, group shelters that have high-velocity air-intake fans would have to have filters on the air-intake system to keep fallout particles out.

How early fallout looks

The most dangerous fallout—early fallout—would consist of radioactive particles that are relatively large and heavy—about the size of table salt or fine sand. The chances are you could see the *particles* although you could not detect the *radiation* from the particles without the use of a special instrument.

Special clothing offers little protection

Fallout radiation would pass through any type of protective clothing that would be practical to wear. Heavy and dense materials, such as earth and concrete, are needed to stop the highly penetrating fallout rays. Certain types of protective clothing could be useful—particularly for emergency workers—in keeping fallout *particles* off the body, but the wearer would not be protected from the *gamma radiation* given off by the particles. The worker would wear the clothing when in a fallout contaminated area, and then discard it or brush and wash it off thoroughly before entering a non-contaminated area.

Little hope in special medicines

Although many experiments have been conducted, there is little likelihood that a pill or any other type of medicine will be developed that can protect people from the effects of fallout radiation, so that shielding from fallout becomes necessary.

Evacuation vs. shelter

Two conditions make pre-attack evacuation of less general value as a protective measure for nuclear attack than it appeared to be a few years ago: the danger of radioactive fallout to unsheltered evacuees, and the decrease in the probable attack-warning time if an enemy should attack with high-speed missiles. However, the problem of mass movement of people in the event of a nuclear attack is still a significant one because plans must be made to get people into shelters rather rapidly. Also, it may be necessary to move people out of severely damaged areas after an attack.

Probable reaction to disaster

Experience has shown that many human beings act cooperatively when disaster strikes, many feel helpless, a few panic. Disaster studies indicate that information, planning, and preparation clearly increase the extent of cooperative and constructive behavior following a disaster.

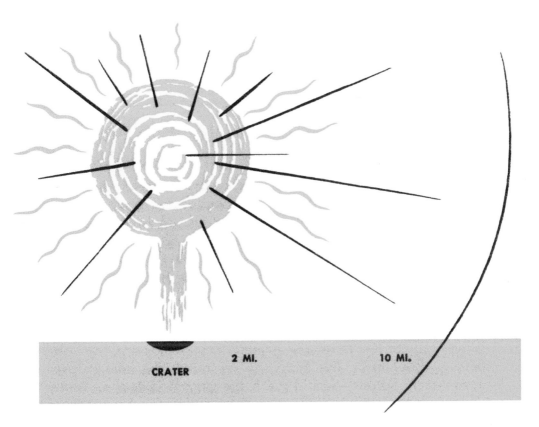

CRATER   2 MI.   10 MI.

A NUCLEAR EXPLOSION:
FIRST, THE BLAST

A five-megaton nuclear weapon explodes with a brilliant flash that lasts about a minute. A quick burst of nuclear and heat radiation emerges from ground zero, the point of the explosion. The spurt of nuclear radiation (*wavy lines extending from the fireball*) is called initial radiation or prompt radiation and kills within a mile or two. The heat rays (*straight lines*) can kill unprotected people up to 10 miles away and may start fires beyond that. The heat rays and initial radiation are followed by a blast wave which starts at more than 2,000 miles an hour, but loses much of its damaging force by about 10 miles out. With the blast wave comes a violent wind which picks up loose objects and bears them outward. In the illustration here, the weapon has burst at ground level, leaving a crater about half a mile across and 200 feet deep. Nearly everything within a radius of a mile of ground zero would be destroyed.

NEXT: FALLOUT
STARTS DESCENDING

As the brilliant fireball rises in the sky, it draws up a vast amount of earth that is melted or vaporized and contaminated by the radioactive residue of the explosion. A little later this material, condensing in the cold upper air like rain or snow, starts falling back to earth because, like ash from a fire, it is heavier than air. It is called fallout because it falls out of the sky, wherever the winds may blow it. You cannot tell from the ground which way it will be carried because its scatter is determined by high-altitude winds, which may be blowing in a different direction from the ground-level winds you can observe. About five miles from the explosion, the heavier particles—early fallout—would reach the ground in half an hour. Twenty miles away, people may have nearly an hour to get ready. One hundred miles away the fallout may not start for four to six hours. All this early fallout, which carries the bulk of the radiation danger, descends in less than 24 hours. The less dangerous lighter particles—delayed fallout—might stay aloft for months.

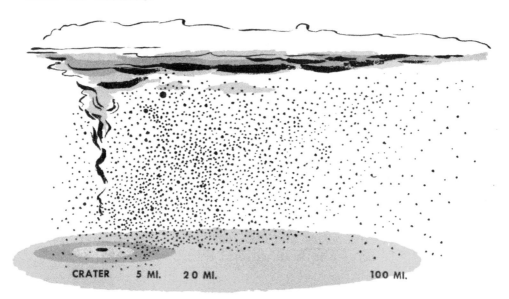

CRATER   5 MI.   2 0 MI.   100 MI.

GROUP ACTION: COMMUNITY SHELTERS

Experience in Europe in World War II and other human experiences under disaster conditions have pointed to distinct advantages of the community or neighborhood fallout shelter when compared with the family shelter. There are several reasons why group shelters are preferable in many circumstances:

1. A larger than family-size group probably would be better prepared to face a nuclear attack than a single family, particularly if some members should be away from home at the time of an attack.

2. There would be more opportunity to find first aid and other emergency skills in a group, and the risk of radiation exposure after an attack could be more widely shared.

3. Community shelters would provide shelter for persons away from their homes at the time of an attack.

4. Group shelters could serve as a focus for integrated community recovery activities in a post-attack period.

5. Group shelters could serve other community purposes, as well as offer protection from fallout following an attack.

For these reasons the Federal Government is undertaking a number of activities—involving guidance, technical assistance, and money—to encourage the development of community fallout shelters. (See "Organizing for Civil Defense.") The overall program, which got underway with the National Shelter Survey, aims at securing group fallout shelters in existing and new structures, stocking them with essential supplies, marking them, and making them available to the public in an emergency.

A model public shelter
and community center

As a model for its hundreds of communities, New York State expects to have a dual-purpose shelter, like the one below, on display at the Westchester County Airport by May of 1962.

Many growing communities or neighborhoods are cramped for space in which small civic groups can hold their meetings. Gregarious teenagers often have no after-school hangout where they can relax with sodas and play the jukebox. This shelter can serve such purposes admirably; here a Scout meeting is going on in one section while adults attend an illustrated lecture in another. Requiring no surface space except for its entrances, the shelter can be built under a school playground or other civic property without interfering with present uses.

The shelter, built of corrugated metal arches buried under several feet of earth, can vary in size. New York's will have three arches, each 10 feet high, 20 feet wide, and 100 feet long. A steel surface door will lead to a corridor-tunnel providing entry to all arches. Arches can be reinforced with metal ribs for extra blast protection.

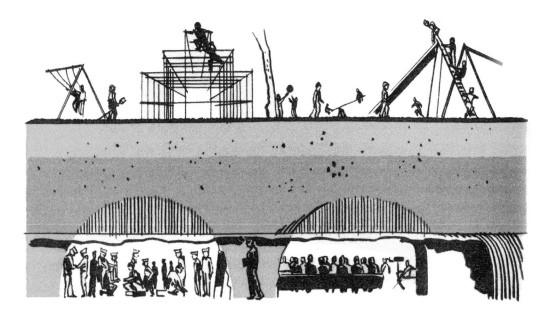

Built-in shelter
in new structures

Added safety against fallout radiation can be built into a new structure without great extra cost. Sometimes the necessary protection can be assured by using the "safety core" design principle illustrated in the school building below. Even though it has no basement, the school house provides a shelter that is also useful for other purposes. The thick-walled central core with concrete-slab roof contains "activity rooms," divided and reinforced by the walls of a library and rest rooms. Projecting baffle walls shield the windows of surrounding classrooms.

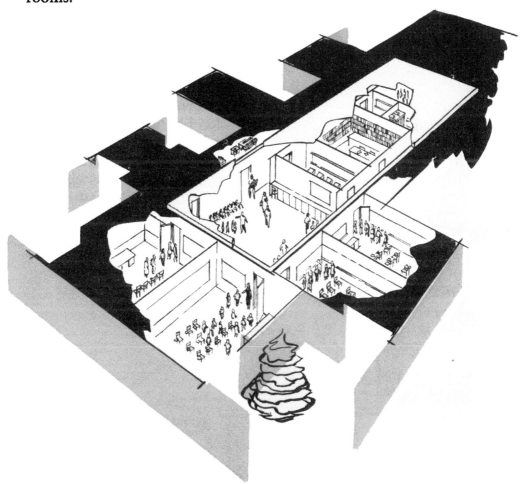

A city building
provides fallout protection

After a nuclear attack, a tall apartment or office building 10 miles or more from the explosion could be one of the safest refuges. In this drawing the people have taken shelter from radioactive fallout in an office building.

Because the gamma rays given off by fallout penetrate much like X-rays, the people taking shelter in the building shown on the opposite page have put as much mass of material as possible between themselves and the particles which have settled on the roof, ground, and other horizontal surfaces. Above ground, they have gone to the middle of the building; below ground, they have found shielding in a basement corner. Those in the main basement are shielded from radiation by the surrounding earth, by partitions, and by the whole mass of the building above. On the upper floors, people have shielded themselves in the "core" of the building. They have avoided the floor with the setback and terrace because of radiation from the fallout piling up there. (For better protection on any floor, it is advisable to keep below the window-sill level.) Because the tall building shields lower floors from some radiation, people have taken shelter in more rooms on that side. But no one has taken cover on the ground and top floors because the shielding there is inadequate.

INDIVIDUAL ACTION:
FAMILY SHELTERS

Families living in rural or sparsely settled areas may find that family shelters are the only feasible solution to their fallout shelter problem. Others may have personal preferences for family shelters.

There are a number of ways to construct home shelters. Several types are shown here. All of the shelters shown here can be built with about $150 worth of materials or less. If materials, such as the lumber used in a basement lean-to shelter, are available at little or no cost, some persons could build these shelters for considerably less than $150. In all of the shelters, the danger from fallout would be at least 100 times less than to unprotected persons.

This family is building a basement compact shelter of sand-filled concrete blocks. Solid concrete blocks are used for the roof shielding. This type of shelter also could be built of brick or structural tile.

Construction drawings on these and other family shelters can be obtained by following the instructions on the last page of this booklet.

In selecting shielding material for any shelter, sand or earth can be substituted for concrete or brick, but for each inch of solid masonry you need an inch and a half of sand or earth. Adding shielding material to a shelter will improve the protection offered by the shelter, but it also may increase the cost of the shelter.

This sand-filled lean-to basement shelter will accommodate three persons. The house itself gives partial shielding. Sandbags are used to block the end of the shelter.

This backyard plywood shelter can be built partially above ground and mounded over with earth, or be built totally below ground level.

A gravel drain under the shelter and a ditch outside help keep it dry. The family blocks the entrance with sandbags after entering the shelter.

A number of firms have entered the home shelter field. As in any new commercial activity there are abuses. Advertising claims may be misleading; designs and products may be inadequate. Your State and Federal governments will do what they properly can to minimize these abuses, but the most effective discouragement to those taking advantage of the rising interest in home shelters is your caution and shrewdness. You will have the cooperation of the Better Business Bureau, your local Civil Defense director, and of your local, State, and Federal government officials concerned with such matters.

Trade associations that are interested in the shelter construction business have offered their cooperation in making home shelter plans available to the public and in working with others to maintain a high level of business practice. Several of these are listed on the last page of this booklet.

In the event of a nuclear attack, be prepared to live in a shelter as long as two weeks, coming out for short trips only if necessary. Fallout would be most dangerous in the first two days

This prefab backyard shelter for four can be bought for under $150. The price includes the corrugated steel-pipe unit (4-foot diameter), entry and air vent pipes.

after an attack, and even if you were inside a shelter you probably would have absorbed some radiation. Your freedom of action would depend on your radiation exposure during the critical period after the fallout descends. So, never expose yourself unnecessarily to radiation.

This four-person basement-corner shelter is made of curved asbestos-cement sheets which are covered with sandbags. Materials cost about $125.

LAST-MINUTE IMPROVISED MEASURES

In the nuclear age, nobody can guarantee you so many minutes, hours, or days of warning time. An enemy ultimatum might set a deadline; enemy bombers could be tracked while hours away; but enemy missiles could arrived unannounced. However, even the briefest warning you might get by radio or sirens would give you the precious, live-saving time to act.

The two public warning signals are:

A 3- to 5-minute STEADY TONE, meaning, turn on your radio for directions from local authorities.

A 3-minute WARBLING TONE or SHORT BLASTS, meaning take cover immediately.

There are at least two situations that could increase the severity of the danger you would face: A plan of action but no time to put it into effect, or time to act but no plan of action—no shelter, for example.

A plan but no time

Your first warning of nuclear attack could be the flash of an explosion. Don't look at it. Quick action during the next few seconds could save your life.

If you are inside, dive under or behind the nearest desk, table, sofa or other piece of sturdy furniture. Try to get in a shadow;

If you have no basement, you can improvise a shelter by digging a trench next to the house, and making a lean-to structure with house doors. Pile the dirt from the trench and other heavy objects on top of the doors and at the sides for as much radiation shielding as possible.

it will help shade you from the heat. Lie curled on your side with your hands over the back of your neck, knees tucked against your chest. Stay away from windows, or turn your back to them—they admit heat rays and also may shatter.

If you are outside, run into a building and assume the same curled-up position. If possible, face a corner.

If you cannot get into a building, seek the lowest, most protected spot, such as a ditch, gutter or depression in a lawn. Lie in the curled position. Face away from loose or breakable objects.

If you are far enough away from the explosion you may feel no effect at all. But stay put for five minutes to be sure. By then the blast effects will have passed or lost their force. You will have at least half an hour to find fallout protection.

Time but no plan

If you should receive warning of an attack but do not have a plan of action—no shelter to go to, for example—your first actions should be to guard against the hazards of fires set by the heat of a nuclear explosion. Get rid of such quick burning things as oily rags, curtains, and lampshades. Get rid of old newspapers and magazines, or stack them in the basement if you plan to improvise a fallout shelter there. Shut off main electric and gas lines until the fire danger has passed. If your house has venetian blinds, lower and shut them to bar flying glass and screen out some of the blast's fierce heat. Fill buckets, sinks, a bathtub, and other containers with water.

Then turn your attention to fallout protection. There are six general guidelines to keep in mind for improvising last-minute fallout protection:

1. A basement is usually better than aboveground floors, particularly in private residences. (In large commercial or civic buildings, however, the central areas of middle floors could offer good protection.)

2. A corner of a basement that is below ground level is better than the center of the basement.

3. On aboveground floors, improvise shelter away from outside walls.

4. When improvising shelter, keep it small. Concentrate the shielding mass immediately around and above you to conserve construction time.
5. Stay away from windows and outside doorways. They are weak points in your fallout shield. Also, windows could be shattered many miles beyond the severe blast damage area of a nuclear explosion.
6. If caught in the open, try to get to some substantial structure, such as a large commercial or civic building, a tunnel, or cave. If none of these is readily available, look for a culvert, underpass or ditch—anything that will get you below ground level—and improvise a shelter.

This man is improvising a fallout shelter in a basement corner by stacking heavy material on and at the open sides of a sturdy table. Piling dirt and other heavy material in the basement window wells will improve his margin of protection.

SHELTER SUPPLIES

Not every item on this chart is vital to life. (The most essential ones are outlined in color.) But even though you might be able to leave your shelter briefly after a day or two, you should prepare to be *completely* self-sustaining for at least two weeks.

EATING UTENSILS AND FOOD

EATING UTENSILS

MEASURING CUP

PAPER PLATES

PAN

CUPS

NAPKINS

WATER

BOTTLE OPENER

CAN OPENER

POCKET KNIFE

FOOD AND CONTAINERS

CLOTHING AND BEDDING

SEWING KIT

SLEEPING BAGS

BLANKETS

EXTRA CLOTHING

SANITATION AND MEDICAL SUPPLIES

DISINFECTANT

GARBAGE CAN

PAPER TOWELS

FIRST AID KIT

SANITARY NAPKINS

EMERGENCY TOILET

TOILET PAPER

HUMAN WASTE

NEWSPAPERS

SOAP

PLASTIC AND PAPER BAGS

The one essential is water; most people can live no more than four days without it. The minimum for a shelter is one quart of fluid per person per day; if space is available near the shelter, a gallon of water a day per person would provide for your comfort, including washing.

Some items, such as tools, should be kept handy but need not be inside the shelter itself.

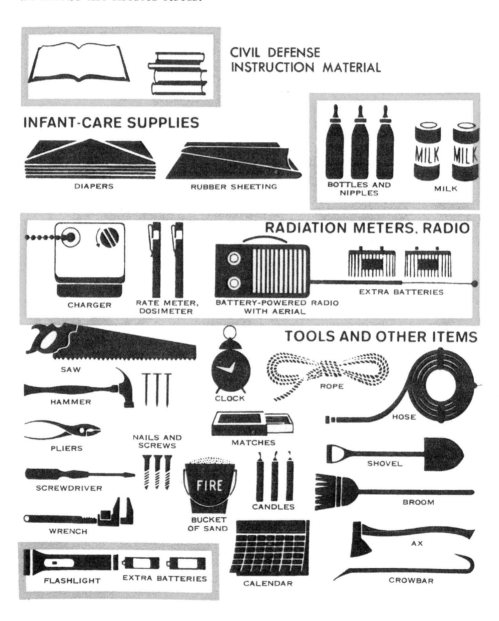

CIVIL DEFENSE INSTRUCTION MATERIAL

INFANT-CARE SUPPLIES

DIAPERS

RUBBER SHEETING

BOTTLES AND NIPPLES

MILK

RADIATION METERS, RADIO

CHARGER

RATE METER, DOSIMETER

BATTERY-POWERED RADIO WITH AERIAL

EXTRA BATTERIES

TOOLS AND OTHER ITEMS

SAW

HAMMER

NAILS AND SCREWS

CLOCK

ROPE

HOSE

PLIERS

MATCHES

SHOVEL

SCREWDRIVER

FIRE

CANDLES

BROOM

WRENCH

BUCKET OF SAND

AX

FLASHLIGHT

EXTRA BATTERIES

CALENDAR

CROWBAR

EMERGENCY

HOUSEKEEPING

Following is a checklist of preparations for, and best ways of, living in close confinement for the two days to two weeks when a shelter may have to be your home. Also included is a resume of the first aid information you may need.

Water

It is more vital than food. Humans can live on a quart of water or other fluid a day, but an allowance of a gallon is far more comfortable, especially in a warm shelter.

Store water in five-gallon or larger containers to conserve space. If you use small glass containers, seal them well and pack them with newspapers or wadding to prevent breakage. Some may want to test their stored water for smell and taste every three months, but it is not necessary for health. Odorous as it might become, it will still be usable in an emergency. Announcements on your radio may tell you whether local water supplies are safe. If they are not, you can preserve a considerable safe water supply in your house by closing the water shut-off valve leading in from the street. The water in toilet flush tanks, pipes, hot water tanks, and similar home sources is drinkable.

Unless authorities have pronounced it safe, try to avoid using water from outside the house or open sources (lakes, reservoirs) after the attack without purifying it. Germs or radioactive material, or both, may get into water. Cloudy or unclear water should first be strained through a paper towel or several thicknesses of clean cloth, or else be allowed to settle in a deep container and then siphoned off. After that, it may be freed of germs with water purification tablets, obtainable at drug and sporting goods stores, or by boiling vigorously for a few minutes, or by adding 20 drops of iodine to a gallon of clear water or 40 drops to a gallon of cloudy water. Then let it stand for 30 minutes. Liquid household bleaches of the sodium hypochlorite type can also be used. The label usually gives instructions.

Radiation in itself does not affect water. It is only if the radioactive particles themselves get into water that the water becomes dangerous. There are effective ways to decontaminate water containing radioactive particles. The particles can be removed by the simple filtering process with paper or cloth that

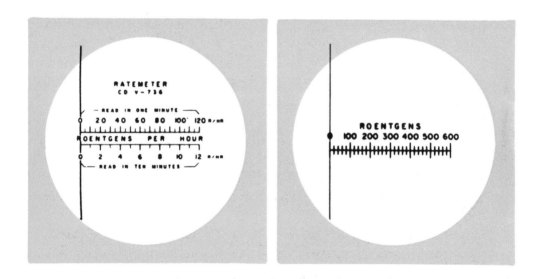

Enlarged view of a ratemeter scale. This particular model must be exposed to radiation for certain specific times to measure the dose rate (intensity) of radiation.

Enlarged view of a dosimeter scale. The instrument is used to measure the total amount of radiation to which a person has been exposed.

was described earlier, or by running the water through one of the devices that are sold to soften water for home use. Perhaps an easier way would be to mix a handful of clay soil with each gallon of water and allow it to settle out over a period of a day.

Radiation meters

Because gamma rays, like X-rays, are not detected by any of the five senses, each shelter should have some simple instruments to detect and measure them. Instruments developed specifically for home use can be ordered through department stores and other retail outlets. Having these instruments does not automatically provide you with simple solutions to problems of radiation exposure since the relations between dose rate, total dose, time, radioactive decay, etc., must be learned. Instructions will be available, however, on how to interpret the instrument readings. If these are studied and understood in advance, the instruments can be of great value in intelligently planning your action in a fallout situation.

A ratemeter will tell what the intensity of the radiation is. It is similar to a speedometer in a car except that it measures roentgens per hour rather than miles per hour. Thus, from a ratemeter reading made just outside the shelter, you can get an indication of whether it is safe to leave the shelter for a brief period. The dosimeter will show you the total amount of radiation to which you have been exposed during an emergency period. It is similar to a mileage indicator in a car but it measures total roentgens rather than miles. Carefully study the instructions provided with these instruments by the manufacturer.

At right is a kit of radiation instruments developed specifically for home use—a ratemeter, dosimeter, and charger. Other models are being developed.

Food

Wherever you live—in the country, city apartment, or suburban house—you should keep a two-week supply of food on hand. Large community shelters in existing buildings are going to be stocked by the Federal Government with emergency foods. But for the present, and especially for apartment residents who may have to take quick refuge in the central core or basement of their building, a good plan is to keep handy a box or basket with rations and water.

In planning a two-week supply of food for whatever shelter you will use, bear these things in mind:

Ten thousand calories will be adequate for an adult during an inactive two-week shelter stay. Select familiar foods (they are more heartening and acceptable during times of stress) and food that will last for months without refrigeration and can be served without cooking. Suggestions: canned meat, fish, poultry, beans, peas and fruits; cereals and tinned baked goods; cheese spreads, peanut butter and jellies with crackers; evaporated or dried milk.

Pick cans and packages of a size suitable to your family's needs for one meal; this prevents spoilage and offers you greater daily variety. Keep all foods in their original containers. Those that do not come in cans should be wrapped and tape-sealed in polyethylene sheets. Write the date of purchase on cans or packages, and use oldest purchases first.

After a nuclear attack, food stored indoors should be safe to eat. That is especially true of food in freezers and refrigerators, which should, of course, be kept closed as much as possible. Eat the perishable foods first, especially if electricity and gas are cut off. Bread is still edible even when moldy; sour milk is drinkable. Fruits and vegetables with "rotten" spots cut out are safe to eat; if they have been exposed to fallout, wipe, wash and peel them, disposing of wash-water and peelings outside the shelter.

Throw out canned foods if bubbles appear in the juices, even though they smell all right. In an emergency, most canned and packaged animal foods can be eaten by humans without harm.

A hand-operated air blower, like this one at the left, would provide ample ventilation for any underground family shelter. Other models are being developed.

Ventilation

Fresh air is more vital than food and water. A basement home shelter will get its air via door cracks and other crevices through which fallout particles are unlikely to drift. But well-sealed community shelters and home underground ones will need ventilation systems because even at rest a person should have at least three cubic feet of air a minute.

In many home underground shelters a three-inch intake pipe is installed to suck in fresh air by means of a hand-operated blower that is cranked periodically, and an exhaust pipe is set up to vent stale air. The air-intake pipe should extend at least a foot above the ground, and have a weather cap over it to keep out fallout particles.

Community shelters should have an air filter to remove particles that may get into the ventilation system. Since this filter may collect radioactive material, the people in the shelter should be shielded from it. No blower is necessary for the outlet or exhaust pipe because of the pressure created within the shelter by the intake blower. In smaller shelters the outlet pipe may be unnecessary because air would leave through cracks around the door. Blowers are available at hardware stores.

Radiation sickness

The principal ailment unique to nuclear warfare is radiation sickness. Its severity depends on the amount of radiation to which a person is exposed and on the length of the exposure time. That is because the body can take a certain amount of radiation damage and repair it without serious permanent injury. It is only when one gets too much too fast that sickness or possibly death may result. Radiation sickness is *not* contagious, regardless of how much exposure the victim has had. It is important to know that many of its symptoms may appear in anyone subjected at any time to anxiety and great stress.

Symptoms of three degrees of radiation sickness are: *Mild*—the especially sensitive person will show some nausea, lack of appetite and fatigue within a few hour after exposure. He should rest but can continue normal activities. Recovery will be rapid. *Moderate*—the same symptoms appear, but well within two hours of exposure, and more markedly. Vomiting and even prostration may occur. By the third day, recovery may seem complete, but symptoms may recur in the next days or weeks. *Severe*—again, all the early symptoms show up and may vanish after a few days. But after a week or more, fever, mouth soreness and diarrhea may appear; gums and mouth may ulcerate and bleed; and, in about the third week, the patient's hair may start to fall out. Recovery may take seven to eight weeks. When exposure has been overwhelming, death comes in hours or weeks.

Treat symptoms in this way: General rest. Aspirin for headache. Motion-sickness tablets for nausea. Liquids as soon as possible for diarrhea and vomiting, but not until vomiting has stopped (ideally, one teaspoon of table salt to one quart of cool water, to be sipped slowly). For sore mouth, this solution can be used as a mouthwash.

First aid

Since doctors, medical supplies, and other aids may not be available to everyone for days or even weeks in some areas, it is important for at least one adult in every family to know standard first aid. Civil Defense units, in cooperation with Red Cross Chapters, give courses you can take. In addition, a new training course in Medical Self Help, with a reference handbook, contains valuable information on what to do should professional medical care be unavailable to you because of emergency conditions.

There are five basic first-aid rules that *everyone* should know. They are:

How to stop bleeding. The average adult body contains only six quarts of blood; the loss of one quart is serious, so bleeding has priority over all other emergencies. Apply pressure to the wound at once—with your hand if nothing else is available, although a bandage, clean cloth, or sanitary napkin will help prevent infection. But don't waste time looking for them. Don't wash the wound. Apply pressure hard and fast, bringing the edges of the wound together if you can. You may have to continue the pressure for 30 minutes.

Never apply the old-fashioned tourniquet except as a last resort. It may cost the patient his limb.

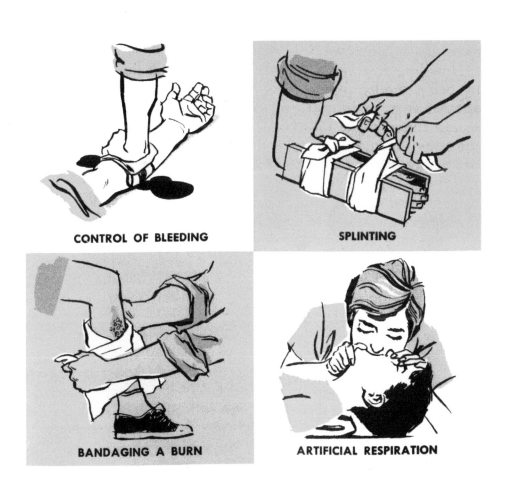

CONTROL OF BLEEDING

SPLINTING

BANDAGING A BURN

ARTIFICIAL RESPIRATION

Breathing difficulties. Getting air into the victim's lungs fast is vital. Remove throat obstructions such as mucus, debris, a jarred-loose denture. If he is breathing, place him on his stomach, head to one side so that blood or secretions will not flow into air passages. If he is not breathing, apply mouth-to-mouth respiration. Tilt victim's head back to "sword-swallower" position (a blanket or pillow under shoulders will help), pinch his nose shut (*see drawing*), seal your open mouth over his, inhale deeply through your nose and exhale deeply into his mouth 12 to 16 times a minute for an adult, 20 for a child. Continue this for two hours, even if life seems extinct, before giving up. As he revives, adjust your breathing rhythm to his.

If the patient has a chest wound, cover it with an airtight dressing.

Handling fractures. Simple bone fractures show themselves by being tender to touch, or by the unnatural shape of the affected part, or by swelling and change in skin color. Compound fractures are indicated by broken skin, sometimes with the bone protruding. Splint the fracture wherever the patient lies before moving him, firmly supporting the broken limb.

Burns. Light burns (reddening of the skin) need not be covered, and can be treated with pain relievers or left alone. Deeper burns, where blisters and especially destruction of tissue under the skin occur, should be covered with a clean dressing. No ointments or salves should be used. Fluid that oozes from the burn and forms a crust is a good dressing in itself. Don't puncture blisters unless they are likely to break; in this case make a small slit at the edge.

If the burns are severe, get the victim to drink a salt solution if possible (one level teaspoon salt to one quart of water) in small amounts. A gallon during the first 24 hours is not too much.

Comfort. Reassuring the patient in a confident way is vital. Move him only if necessary and then as little as possible. It may be useful to place the patient in a slightly head-down position. Do not give alcoholic drinks as a stimulant.

Sanitation

In the limited space of a shelter, good sanitation is not merely a matter of comfort; it could be a matter of life or death. The familiar, old-fashioned diseases can still kill as surely as blast or radiation, and intimate living makes contagion easy. Probably the biggest single problem is the disposal of human waste, which can spread such diseases as typhoid, dysentery, and diarrhea.

The most elemental device is a metal pail with a tight cover. A better expedient, especially where elderly persons are involved, is to make a commode by cutting the seat out of a chair and placing the pail under it. In either case a supply of plastic bags, obtainable at department stores, is needed, a bag being placed in the pail with its top overlapping the pail rim. A small amount of disinfectant (creosol or household bleach) can help control odors and insect breeding.

A larger can with a cover, such as a garbage can, should be available to store the plastic bags after use. After two days, the container can be placed outside the shelter. At a later time, bury such waste under one to two feet of earth. Garbage should be handled and disposed of in the same way. It is best wrapped first in several thicknesses of newspaper, which absorbs some moisture and helps hold down odors. Then put it in a covered can.

Control of vermin

Measures to control vermin would be vital in the event of an attack, but some measures can be taken now. The shelter area should be painted or sprayed with a five per cent solution of DDT or other insecticides containing chlordane, dieldrin, Diazinon, or ronnel—taking the usual precautions against inhalation or skin contact. Repeat every few months. Lice and other body-infesting insects can be eliminated by dusting with a 10 per cent DDT dust which should be kept on the body and in clothing for 24 hours. The shelter should be stocked with screening material, a fly swatter, mouse and rat traps. Do not use spray insecticides in an occupied shelter; there is danger of explosion or of injuring eyes and lungs.

FIRST STEPS TOWARD RECOVERY

The world and your community would be shattered by a nuclear war. Normal services would be disrupted; essential skills could be in short supply; equipment you had taken for granted might not be available. You would face the aftermath of a catastrophe, but if there had been previous planning, you need not face it alone.

Using community resources

As in the case of natural disasters, community action is by far the best way to do all that must be done to recover from a nuclear attack. Local governments have at hand many organized units, such as the police and fire departments, the county road commission and the health department, whose survivors can serve as a hard core for organized recovery actions immediately after people can emerge from shelters. Government agencies, military units, and other organizations, such as construction companies and the repairmen of the public utilities, would help to repair damage and restore service as soon as possible—as they have in past natural disasters. But many more helpers would be needed. Wherever you might be, in a community or family shelter, your help would be needed. If your community is lucky and receives little fallout, you may be needed to help a neighboring community.

The communities that are well organized and have planned their recovery actions would be able to return to tolerable living conditions in the shortest time. The first job in this would be to clean up pre-selected areas to make them safe for living outside of shelters. The initial action may well originate with organized units in community shelters—from the basement of the city hall, from a shelter at a school—or it could come from groups in several shelters working together. As groups, they would have more of the manpower, equipment, and communications needed to start the job.

Getting rid of fallout

The process of removing fallout particles from exposed surfaces and disposing of the particles in places where they cannot harm people is called radiological decontamination. Paved areas could be decontaminated with firehoses or street flushers, using high-pressure nozzles, and with motorized street sweepers. Roofs could be decontaminated with fire hoses. Unpaved areas could be decontaminated by scraping off or plowing under a thin top layer of soil. This could be done with large earth-moving equipment—such as motorized scrapers and motor graders—on large open areas, and with bulldozers, tractor scrapers, shovels and wheelbarrows on smaller areas around houses and trees. Another method would be to cover a contaminated area with clean earth.

In decontaminating paved areas, crews could flush the particles into storm drains or into ditches, where the particles could be covered with clean earth or picked up and hauled to a dumping area. The scrapings from the unpaved areas could be dumped in a pile about 100 feet from occupied areas, or hauled away. The dumping area might be a gully, refuse area, or even a vacant lot roped off at a safe distance.

Since the most effective and rapid methods of decontamination would involve the use of crews and equipment working in large areas, the best places to start the decontamination are likely to be at schools, shopping centers and downtown areas, and at parks and open fields where large equipment can operate.

It is vital that communities set aside in advance many rallying points where people can meet to start work after an attack. If you are in a home shelter and have a ratemeter, you should wait until the radiation level has fallen to a point where you can go out for about an hour without receiving more than a few roentgens. You could use this time to go to your local school, shopping area or other designated gathering place and join with your neighbors in community decontamination efforts.

If you do not have a radiation instrument, stay in shelter until you are assured, by radio, by contact from local authorities, or by other means, that clean areas are established near you and that it is safe to proceed there.

In areas of heavy fallout where the first decontamination actions can be started, if well organized, within the second week after attack, there is relatively little danger from fallout particles getting on people doing cleanup work—especially if normal habits of personal cleanliness are maintained. The most likely articles of clothing to pick up fallout particles are shoes, so keep them brushed clean.

On a farm

If you live on a farm, your pre-fallout preparations will have a lot to do with your cleaning up afterward.

You should place as much of your livestock and produce in barns as you can. A normally filled hayloft affords some shielding from fallout radiation for animals below. Farm machinery, troughs, wells, and any produce you cannot get into barns should be covered with tarpaulins. You should store as much water in covered containers as you can, taking the precautions already outlined.

Afterward, any livestock exposed to fallout could be washed or brushed to remove fallout particles. Water from wells and streams would be safe for animal use. Even water standing in a pond could be use since fallout particles would settle to the bottom. Pond water could be made even safer by stirring up a clay bottom and then letting it settle out. Feed and fodder stored under cover should be used first. If no other feed is available, animals could be turned out to pasture after a few days when the radioactivity has decreased.

Farm animals and poultry would be an important source of human food and they should not be allowed to sicken and die from thirst and starvation. Animals which have been exposed to early fallout or which have fed on contaminated pastures could be slaughtered and the muscle meat would be fit for human consumption. Internal organs, however, such as the liver and spleen, should not be eaten unless no other food is available. It would be easier to preserve meat on the hoof than on the hook. Hogs and steers could be kept alive even with water and feed containing early fallout particles.

Animals, like humans, can have radiation sickness. If the radiation level in your area indicates that animal sickness may be widespread, you probably will be told and given instructions on slaughtering. Care must be taken in slaughtering to prevent contamination of the carcasses by fallout particles from the hides and digestive tracts.

Chickens and eggs would be a particularly important direct food resource because they are relatively resistant to radiation, especially if they are raised under cover using safe packaged feeds.

Milk from cows that have grazed on contaminated pastures would be radioactive, but in the absence of other food in an emergency, it could be used.

Potatoes, corn, and other field crops exposed to early fallout would be safe to eat after cleaning. Grain that has been covered, as in elevators, would be safe. Threshing would reduce the amount of fallout particles in grain. Threshed grain exposed to fallout could be made safer by washing.

If county agents are available, they can help you decide what crops, pasturage, and methods will be best and safest to use. Seeds of all sorts are quite resistant to radiation and do not require any special protection.

ORGANIZING
FOR CIVIL DEFENSE

Fallout shelter is only one part of a complete Civil Defense Program. The details of a Civil Defense Program may change with changes in the kinds of missiles that might be used against us. But the essential elements of the program remain the same. They consist of a warning system to alert the civilian population to an imminent attack; a system of shelters equipped and provisioned to furnish protection against those effects of an attack for which protection is feasible—i.e., radioactive fallout; and a system to provide training and equipment, so that the survivors can monitor the effects of the attack and carry out the tasks of decontamination, fire fighting, rescue, and reconstruction, that would be necessary to restore a functioning society.

An effective civil defense requires the participation of every citizen. It calls for advance planning at every level of government—local, State, and national. This planning must be flexible enough to adapt itself to changes in enemy weapons and tactics. It must be comprehensive enough to cover people living under widely different conditions from ranch houses, to apartment buildings, to frame cottages.

Responsibilities

The Federal Civil Defense Act puts the responsibility for civil defense jointly on the Federal Government and the States. Until this year, there has been little interest, and less money available for civil defense, so that it has not been necessary to define responsibilities precisely. Now we have launched a major program. Under this program, the Federal Government has assumed four responsibilities: First, to keep track of the nature of the threat which the Civil Defense Program must be designed to meet; second, to prepare information about the threat and how it can be met; third, to bear a major part of the costs of certain kinds of civil defense activities, where such sharing will stimulate State and local and private activities; and, fourth, to provide technical assistance through State and local channels for civil defense planning.

Your State and local governments, on the other hand, have the operating responsibility for civil defense. An individual must be able to look to some agency of his State or local Government for advice and assistance on civil defense planning, just as he looks to them for police and fire protection services. By the same token, the responsibility for organizing community civil defense protection falls on the States and, through them, on local government units. Because the job is an extraordinarily difficult one, the Federal Government is preparing to assist the States with technical help and matching funds for certain programs.

The key element in our new program is the provision of fallout shelter. We expect community shelters to protect a large part of the population; but we recognize that many families, because of their location or individual preferences, will choose family fallout shelters. The Federal Government will join with States and communities, in a variety of ways, to help provide fallout shelter.

National shelter survey

We have already taken the first step towards a realistic Civil Defense Program by launching the National Shelter Survey. The survey will identify the approximately 50 million shelter spaces that are now available in existing buildings, tunnels, subways, and other structures to provide protection from radioactive fallout.

Many of these spaces in the central areas of large population centers would be exposed to destruction by blast and fire in the event of a nuclear attack. But the pattern of attack cannot be predicted, and existing shelter is more widely distributed in relation to population than appears to the casual observer. Further, this space is immediately available, and the cost of identification, marking, and stocking is less than $4 per space.

All such shelter spaces, accommodating 50 or more people, and which would be open to the public in an emergency, will be marked and stocked with essential food, water, first-aid kits, and radiation detection instruments.

Proposed shelter incentive program

The President plans to seek funds from the Congress to support a Federal Shelter Incentive Program in which the Federal Government would meet a substantial part of the costs of providing fallout shelters in schools, hospitals, and other public welfare institutions. The program is designed to encourage the construction of fallout shelter in these essential community facilities. Many of these institutions are in excellent locations for group fallout shelters, but many of them have very limited resources of their own to pay for shelter construction.

The Federal Shelter Incentive Program would help to fill this gap. The plan provides a Federal grant of something less than actual cost for every shelter space meeting approved standards, and created in public, or private non-profit institutions, engaged in health, education, or welfare activities. A substantial number of these shelters would be dual purpose, serving a useful peacetime community purpose, in addition to offering protection from radioactive fallout in the event of attack.

In order to qualify for incentive payments, each shelter would have to accommodate a minimum of 50 people, and would have to be open for public use in time of emergency. Upon completion, each shelter would be identified by the continuing operations of the National Shelter Survey, and would be marked and stocked with food, water, first-aid kits, and radiation detection instruments. All schools, colleges, hospitals, clinics, and welfare institutions would be eligible for shelter incentive payments, provided they were operated by a State or local government unit, or by a private non-profit organization.

The Federal Shelter Incentive Program, together with the Federal Shelter Survey, is expected to stimulate a good deal of additional construction and modification of shelter space. The primary responsibility for exploiting the exemplary effect of the Federal programs lies with the State and local civil defense organizations. Their success will depend largely on their ability to organize a local civil defense program in each community. This effort includes not only the provision of shelter, but an adequate system of warning, of radiological monitoring, and of training and information on survival techniques.

Other federal programs

Every citizen needs to know how he will be warned of imminent attack, where he will take shelter, how he should behave in the shelter, and what he should expect when he emerges from it. In addition, as many citizens as possible should be trained in the techniques of shelter management, radiological monitoring, decontamination, rescue, fire fighting, and restoring essential service.

Besides helping to build shelters, the Federal Government will help in building these other elements of the Civil Defense Program in a number of ways.

The Federal Government helps to provide warning against an attack. The National Warning System carries the warning signal from the Headquarters of the North American Air Defense Command to State warning points. From these points the States send the warning to local warning systems. The Office of Civil Defense is studying national installation of a new warning system, the NEAR System, which would bring the warning into every home with electric power. The NEAR system operates through signal generators placed in the electrical power grid. These generators would be actuated directly by the National Warning System, and in turn, actuate buzzers plugged or wired into home electrical circuits.

The Federal Government is providing equipment for 50,000 radiological monitoring stations, and is training operators for this equipment. The eventual plan calls for 150,000 of these monitoring points to be established in selected community shelters and tied into a control point at the local emergency operating center.

The job of educating every citizen on the results of thermonuclear attack, and what he can do about it, is necessarily the responsibility of State and local civil defense organizations. So is the job of giving specific training to the literally hundreds of thousands of volunteer workers who must be prepared to undertake decontamination, rescue work, firefighting, first aid, and restoration of necessary services. The Federal Government has available a wide range of informational and instructional literature, including course material, technical manuals, and training aids. It also conducts schools to which States may send civil defense operating officials and civil defense instructors. These instructors can then conduct technical training at the local level.

These Federal schools will offer instructor-training courses in shelter management, radiological officer training, radiological detection, civil defense director-training, civil defense operations and plans. This training is provided at Federal expense, and the Federal Government helps pay travel costs to and from the schools. The training materials will be prepared and packaged for the instructor's use in his home State.

The Federal Government, through the Department of Health, Education, and Welfare, also provides instructor training and instructional material for an adult education course in the elements of civil defense, which is currently being conducted in 15 States, and will be extended to cover 35 States by next summer. The President plans to seek funds from the Congress to cover the entire country.

Shelter, warning, radiological monitoring, training and education are all parts of a total community civil defense program. The responsibility for integrating these parts, and relating the whole to the needs and capabilities of the community, necessarily falls on the State and local civil defense organizations. The Federal Government is prepared to help in major ways. As has been indicated, it has already begun, through the National Shelter Survey, to make civil defense a reality.

Basement Sand-Filled Lumber Lean-To Shelter

GENERAL INFORMATION

This shelter is designed to provide protection from the effects of radioactive fallout in the belowgrade basement of an existing structure. Its advantages are low cost, simplicity of construction, general availability of materials, and the fact that it may be easily disassembled.

TECHNICAL SUMMARY

Space and Occupancy.—This shelter design will provide 45 square feet of area and approximately 128 cubic feet of space. It will house three persons. The shelter length can be increased by increments of 4-foot panels. The height may be increased by the use of more materials. This

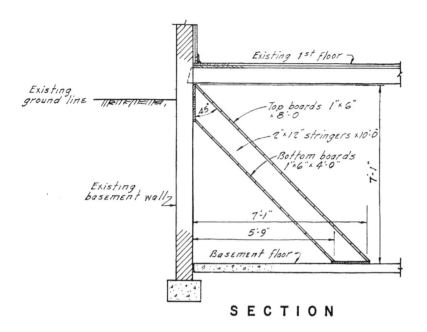

Existing 1st floor

Existing ground line

45°

Top boards 1"×6" ×8'-0"

2"×12" stringers ×10'-0"

Bottom boards 1"×6"×4'-0"

Existing basement wall

7'-1"

7'-1"

5'-9"

Basement floor

S E C T I O N

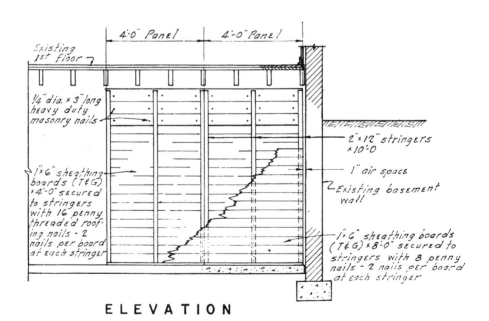

4'-0" Panel   4'-0" Panel

Existing 1st floor

1/4" dia. × 3" long heavy duty masonry nails

1"×6" sheathing boards (T&G) ×4'-0" secured to stringers with 16" penny threaded roofing nails - 2 nails per board at each stringer

2"×12" stringers ×10'-0"

1" air space

Existing basement wall

1"×6" sheathing boards (T&G) ×8'-0" secured to stringers with 8 penny nails - 2 nails per board at each stringer

E L E V A T I O N

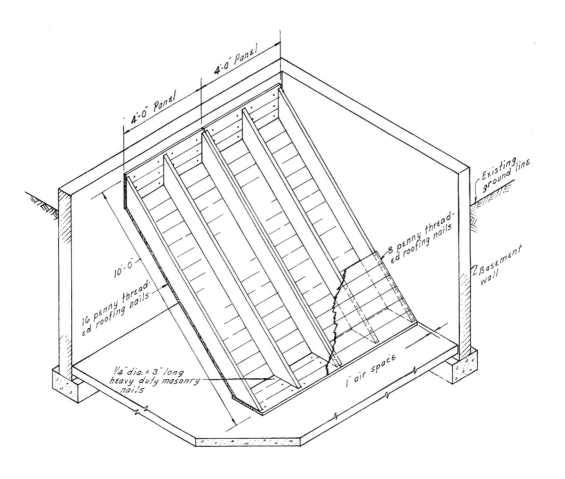

ISOMETRIC VIEW

increase will be limited by basement height and handling of the panels.

Availability and Cost of Materials.—The materials necessary to construct this shelter should be available for a total cost of less than $75 from retail lumberyards.

Fallout Protection Factor.—The shelter is designed to provide a protection factor of at least 100 in most residences.

Blast Protection.—Although this shelter was designed primarily to provide fallout protection, it would also provide some protection from flying debris associated with blast.

Ventilation.—Natural ventilation is obtained by omitting two sandbags from the top of the entranceway closure and by leaving a 1-inch gap between the end of the shelter and the basement wall.

Construction Time.—Construction time should not exceed 20 man-hours when all the materials are on hand at the shelter location. The use of precut panels would reduce the erection time.

Structural Life Expectancy.—When this shelter is erected in a dry basement which is kept free of vermin, its life expectancy range should be from 10 to 15 years.

CONSTRUCTION SEQUENCE

1. Brush-coat all surfaces of lumber with water repellant solution; double brush-coat all cut edges. (Optional.)
2. Cut 45° bevels on 2″ x 12″ stringers. Arrange in 4-foot panels. Using sixteenpenny threaded nails, attach bottom boards on the beveled ends first.
3. Fit in and nail remaining bottom boards.
4. Turn this panel rightside-up and place it in its permanent position. Fasten the panel to the wall and floor with heavy duty masonry nails, leaving a 1-inch gap between the end of the shelter and the basement wall.
5. Construct and fasten in sequence as many panels as are to be used.
6. Line the panels with building paper or polyethylene.
7. Using eightpenny nails, begin attaching top boards at the floor first. Keep the spaces thus formed filled with loose sand as the top-board application progresses. (Building paper or polyethylene sheet should also be applied between the sand and top boards.)
8. Thirty sandbags, each filled with 30 pounds of sand, should be placed in the shelter for emergency closure of entranceway.

BILL OF MATERIALS

(To shelter 3 persons)

Item	Quantity
2″ x 12″ x 10′ rough or surfaced lumber	6 pieces.
1″ x 6″ x 4′ rough or surfaced lumber	50 pieces.
1″ x 6″ x 8′ rough or surfaced lumber (for top covering)	20 pieces.
¼″ diameter x 3″ long heavy-duty masonry nails	2 pounds.
Sixteenpenny threaded roofing nails	6 pounds.
Eightpenny threaded roofing nails	3 pounds.
Dry sand	5½ tons.
Sandbags	30.
Building paper or polyethylene sheet	150 square feet.
Water repellent* (5 percent pentachlorophenol or equal) toxic to wood-destroying fungi and insects.	1 quart.

*Optional.

Basement Corrugated Asbestos-Cement Lean-To Shelter

GENERAL INFORMATION

This shelter is designed to provide low-cost protection from the effects of radioactive fallout. It is intended to be installed belowgrade in a basement area. Its principal advantages are availability of low-cost materials, adaptability to the dimensions of most basements, ease of construction, and it can be disassembled readily.

TECHNICAL SUMMARY

Space and Occupancy.—The lean-to shelter interior has over 40 square feet of area and over 120 cubic feet of space and will house three persons. Its length may be extended by adding sections.
Availability and Cost of Materials.—Materials may be purchased from building materials retailers. Many of these have this shelter in kit

53

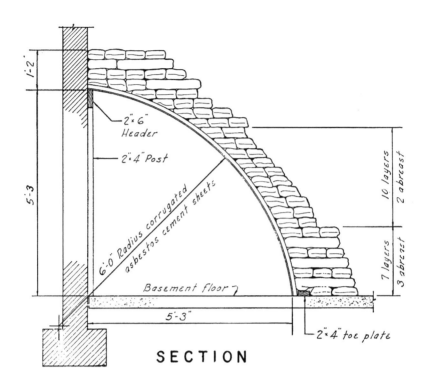

1'-2"

2"× 6"
Header

2"× 4" Post

5'-3"

6'-0" Radius corrugated
asbestos cement sheets

10 layers
2 abreast

7 layers
3 abreast

Basement floor

5'-3"

2"× 4" toe plate

SECTION

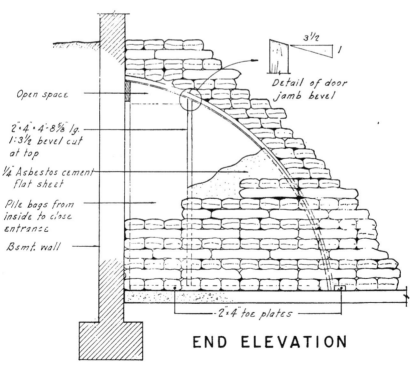

3¹/₂

1

Detail of door
jamb bevel

Open space

2"× 4"× 4'-8⅝" lg.
1:3½ bevel cut
at top

¼" Asbestos cement
flat sheet

Pile bags from
inside to close
entrance

Bsmt. wall

2"× 4" toe plates

END ELEVATION

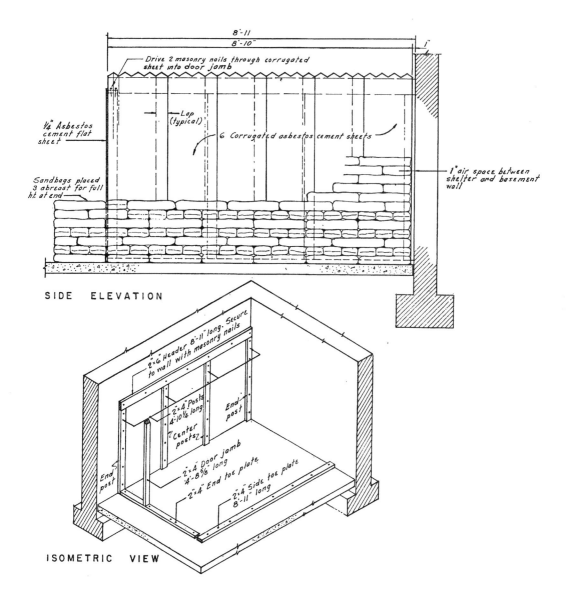

SIDE ELEVATION

ISOMETRIC VIEW

form at a price of about $125. The entire kit is transportable in an average-sized station wagon and can be carried through standard-sized doorways, hallways, and window openings.

Fallout Protection Factor.—The shelter is designed to provide a protection factor of at least 100 in most residences.

Blast Protection.—Although this shelter was designed primarily to provide fallout protection, it would also provide some protection from flying debris associated with blast.

Ventilation.—Natural ventilation is obtained by omitting two sandbags from the top of the entranceway closure and by leaving a 1-inch airgap along the rear wall. (See Construction Sequence, steps 2 and 12.)

Construction Time.—Total construction time is approximately 18 man-hours: 2 hours for construction of the shell and 16 hours for filling and stacking the sandbags.

Structural Life Expectancy.—The range is from 10 to 20 years, depending on the level of humidity in the basement.

CONSTRUCTION SEQUENCE

1. Brush-coat all surfaces of lumber with water-repellent solution; double brush-coat all cut edges.

2. Nail the 2″ x 6″ header and the 2″ x 4″ endposts in place with masonry nails. Leave 1″ airspace for ventilation between end of shelter and basement wall.

3. Mark off header into equal distances and nail centerposts in place.

4. Place curved corrugated asbestos-cement sheets in place with one corrugation overlapping. Rest top of curved sheets on the 2″ x 6″ header.

5. Place 2″ x 4″ toeplate firmly against bottom edge of curved corrugated sheets. Nail toeplate to concrete floor with masonry nails.

6. Nail end toeplate in place.

7. Put the 2″ x 4″ doorjamb in place with the 1 : 3½ bevel on the top end against the curved corrugated sheet. Drive two masonry nails through the corrugated sheet into the doorjamb.

8. Nail precut asbestos-cement flat sheet to doorjamb and toeplate—making sure flat sheet has solid bearing against curved corrugated sheet as well as doorjamb and toeplate.

9. Fill each sandbag with about 30 pounds of sand and tie securely with wire ties.

10. Stack sandbags three abreast in lowest seven layers around the entire length and entrance end of the shelter with every other layer perpendicular to the corrugated sheets. Start at the end of the shelter where the 1-inch airspace occurs and stagger the bags so that all joints are broken, as in brick wall construction. Partly filled bags will be required to form corners and ends.

11. Continue to stack the bags for the next 10 layers along the length and the end of the shelter, leaving the entranceway open. Bags should be placed two abreast and joints staggered. Enough bags should be laid on top of the shelter to provide 14-inch depth.

12. The remaining bags of sand are placed inside the shelter to be stacked in the entranceway for emergency closure. Omit two bags at the entranceway top for ventilation during shelter use.

BILL OF MATERIALS

(To shelter 3 persons)

Item	Quantity
2″ x 4″ x 58¼″ construction grade fir or equal	5 pieces.
2″ x 6″ x 8′11″ construction grade fir or equal	1 piece.
2″ x 4″ x 8′11″ construction grade fir or equal	1 piece.
2″ x 4″ x 56⅝″ construction grade fir or equal (1 : 3½ bevel on one end).	1 piece.
Water repellent (5 percent pentachlorophenol or equal), toxic to wood-destroying fungi and insects.	1 quart.
3″ spiral-type tempered masonry nails	¾ pound.
43½″ x 59½″ x ¼″ asbestos-cement sheet, cut to 6′ radius	1 piece.
Corrugated sheets, asbestos-cement, curved (6′ radius) 21″ wide x 96″ long.	6 sheets.
9″ x 23″ x 0.004″ polyethylene sandbags with wire ties	650.
Dry sand	10 tons.

Basement Concrete Block Shelter

GENERAL INFORMATION

This concrete block basement compact shelter will provide low-cost protection from the effects of radioactive fallout. It is intended to be installed belowgrade in a basement. Its principal advantages are simple design, speed of construction, and ready availability of low-cost materials. By increasing the ceiling height to 6 feet or more, it could also serve as a dual-purpose room.

TECHNICAL SUMMARY

Space and Occupancy.—This shelter has about 52 square feet of area and 260 cubic feet of space and will provide shelter for four persons.

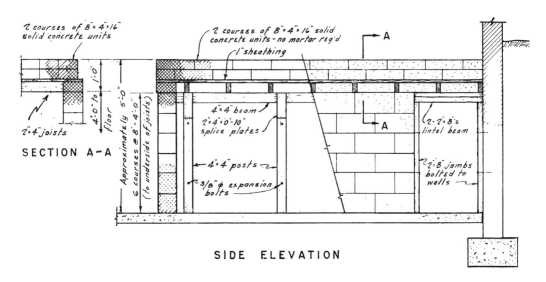

2 courses of 8"×4"×16"
solid concrete units

2 courses of 8"×4"×16" solid
concrete units-no mortar req'd

1" sheathing

A

4'0" to 1'0"
floor

A

2"×4" joists

Approximately 5'-0"

6 courses @ 8"=4'-0"
(to underside of joists)

4"×4" beam

2"×4"×0-10"
splice plates

4"×4" posts

3/8"∅ expansion
bolts

2-2"×8's
lintel beam

2"×8" jambs
bolted to
walls

SECTION A-A

SIDE ELEVATION

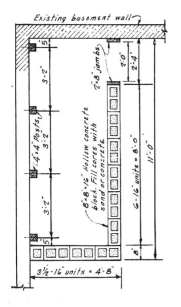

Existing basement wall

2'-0"
2'-4"

5

3'-2"

4"×4" posts
3'-2"

3'-2"

5

2"×8" jambs

8"×8 1/2" Hollow concrete
block. Fill cores with
sand or concrete

6-16" units = 8'-0"

11'-0"

8"

3 1/2-16" units = 4'-8"

FLOOR PLAN

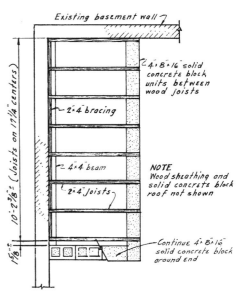

Existing basement wall

4"×8"×16" solid
concrete block
units between
wood joists

2"×4" bracing

4"×4" beam

2"×4" joists

NOTE
Wood sheathing and
solid concrete block
roof not shown

Continue 4"×8"×16"
solid concrete block
around end

10'-2 3/8"± (Joists on 17 1/4 centers)

15 1/8"

ROOF FRAMING PLAN

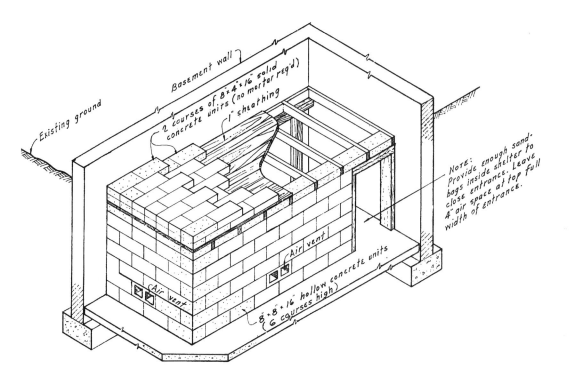

ISOMETRIC VIEW

Availability and Cost of Materials.—Most of the materials required to build this shelter are obtainable at local concrete-block plants and lumber yards. The cost of the materials for the basic shelter is estimated at $75 per shelter.

Fallout Protection Factor.—In most residences, the shelter will provide a protection factor of at least 100.

Blast Protection.—Although this shelter was designed primarily to provide fallout protection, it would also provide some protection from flying debris associated with blast.

Ventilation.—Natural ventilation is provided by the airspace left at the entranceway after emergency closure, and the air vents in the shelter wall.

Construction Time.—Estimated construction time for the basic shelter is less than 20 man-hours.

Structural Life Expectancy.—The life expectancy of the shelter would be about the same as most types of residences.

CONSTRUCTION SEQUENCE

1. Lay out guidelines with chalk on basement floor for shelter walls. (See floor plan.)
2. Lay first course of block in a full bed of mortar. Vary thickness of mortar bed if basement floor is not level.
3. Continue to lay wall blocks. Corner of wall should be built up first, about three or four courses high, before laying blocks in remainder of wall. All blocks should be laid in a full bed of mortar. Where 8-inch blocks are required, cut 16-inch units in half with a hammer and chisel.
4. Fill cores of blocks with sand (or concrete) after three courses have been laid up.
5. Continue procedures indicated above in steps 3 and 4 until walls have been laid up to a height of 4 feet (six courses), and all cores have been filled with sand (or concrete).
6. Brush-coat all surfaces of lumber with water-repellent solution. Double brush-coat all edges. (Optional procedures. Desirable for wood preservation.)
7. Fasten wood posts and doorjambs to existing basement walls and shelter walls with expansion bolts. Use two bolts per post. (See side elevation.)
8. Place wall beam and door lintel beam in position and secure to posts with nails.
9. Place wood joists and bracing in position and secure together with nails. (See roof framing plan.)
10. Place portion of wood sheathing on top of joists. Nail wood sheathing to joists. (See isometric view.)
11. Place solid concrete masonry units on top of wood sheathing. No mortar is required between these units.
12. Continue procedures indicated above in steps 10 and 11 until roof covering has been completed.
13. Bags of sand or additional solid concrete blocks should be stored near entrance for emergency closure, but airspace of at least 4 inches should be left at top of closure for ventilation and air circulation.

BILL OF MATERIALS

(Ceiling height 4 feet)

Item	Quantity
8″ x 8″ x 16″ hollow concrete masonry units*	65.
8″ x 4″ x 16″ solid concrete masonry units*	135.
Mortar (prepared dry mix)	5 cubic feet.
Sand or concrete (for filling cores)	1 ton.
Sandbags	30.
4″ x 4″ x 3′8″ wood posts (structural grade)	4.
2″ x 8″ x 3′8″ wood posts (structural grade)	2.
2″ x 8″ x 2′4″ wood beam (structural grade)	2.
4″ x 4″ x 10′3″ wood beam (structural grade)	1.
1″ wood sheathing	52 board feet.
2″ x 4″ x 4′8″ wood joists (structural grade)	8.
4″ x 4″ x 10′3″ wood beam (structural grade)	8.
2″ x 4″ wood bracing (structural grade)	10 linear feet.
⅜″ x 7″ expansion bolts	12.
Sixteenpenny nails	2 pounds.
Sixpenny nails	2 pounds.
Water repellent (5 percent pentachlorophenol or equal), toxic to wood-destroying fungi and insects.**	1 quart.

*Units should be made with concrete having a density not less than 130 pounds/cubic feet.

**Optional.

Outside Semimounded Plywood Box Shelter

GENERAL INFORMATION

This shelter is designed to provide low-cost protection from the effects of radioactive fallout. Its principal advantages are ready availability of low-cost materials, ease and speed of construction, protection from fallout radiation, and limited blast resistance.

TECHNICAL SUMMARY

Space and Occupancy.—The shelter in this design has 32 square feet of area and 128 cubic feet of space and will house three persons. See *"NOTE"* after "Construction Sequence" for description of a size to house more persons.

Availability and Cost of Materials.—Most of the materials needed to build this shelter are obtainable at lumberyards. The nationwide average for cost of materials is about $75 per shelter, not including ventilation equipment.

Fallout Protection Factor.—A protection factor of about 500 is obtained if the earth cover is 2 feet deep, and a 2-foot thick entranceway shield is formed with bags of sand.

Blast Protection.—The shelter should be able to withstand a limited blast overpressure of 5 pounds per square inch.

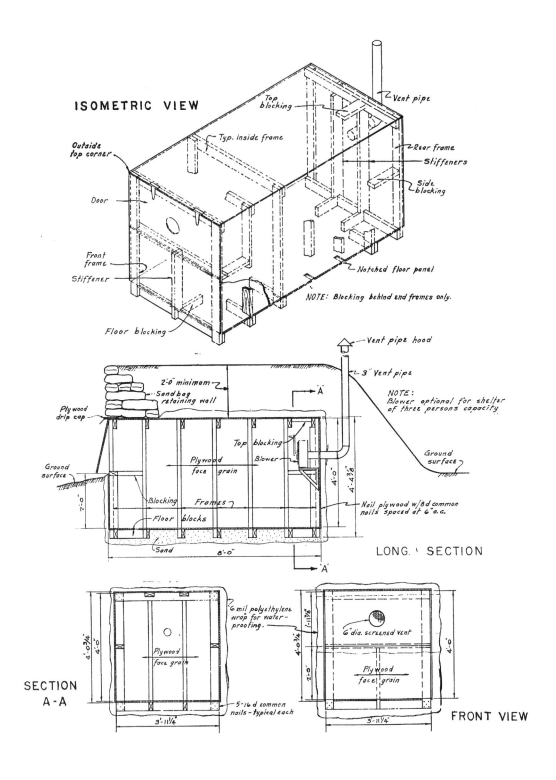

ISOMETRIC VIEW

Top blocking

Vent pipe

Typ. inside frame

Outside top corner

Rear frame

Stiffeners

Side blocking

Door

Front frame

Stiffener

Notched floor panel

NOTE: Blocking behind end frames only.

Floor blocking

Vent pipe hood

2'-0" minimum

Sandbag retaining wall

A

3" Vent pipe

Plywood drip cap

NOTE:
Blower optional for shelter of three persons capacity

Top blocking

Blower

Ground surface

Plywood face grain

Ground surface

2'-0"

Blocking

Frames

Floor blocks

4'-0"

4'-4 3/8"

Nail plywood w/8d common nails spaced at 6" o.c.

Sand

8'-0"

LONG. SECTION

A

6 mil polyethylene wrap for water-proofing.

1'-11 7/8"

6" dia. screened vent

4'-0 3/4"

4'-0"

Plywood face grain

4'-0 3/4"

4'-0"

Plywood face grain

2'-0"

SECTION
A-A

5-16 d common nails - typical each

3'-11 1/4"

3'-11 1/4"

FRONT VIEW

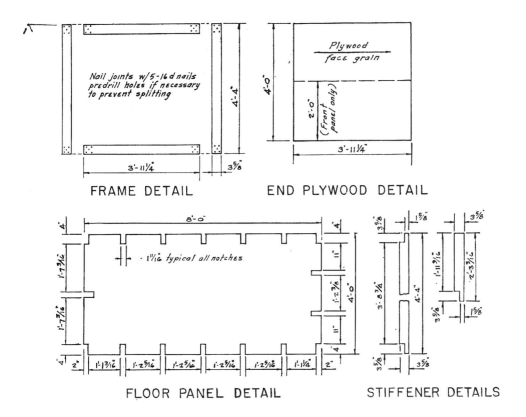

FRAME DETAIL   END PLYWOOD DETAIL

FLOOR PANEL DETAIL   STIFFENER DETAILS

Ventilation.—A 3-inch vent at the rear of the structure provides an essential opening to which a pipe extension can be attached. Hand-operated ventilation equipment should be used for more than three persons. The additional cost may be from $30 to $50. Air is exhausted through the airspace left in the entranceway closure.

Construction Time.—Tests have shown that one man working with simple excavating and construction tools can perform all necessary work in 20 man-hours. This time will be lessened by about 5 hours if lumberyards provide prefabricated plywood panels and sections.

Structural Life Expectancy.—The range is from 5 to 10 years depending on the humidity in the area, drainage characteristics of the terrain, and the effectiveness of the wood treatment (dip preferred) and the plastic wrapping.

CONSTRUCTION SEQUENCE

1. Cut plywood and lumber to size and notch before treating.
2. Dip lumber for 2 minutes or more in water repellent. A trough can be fashioned from a piece of polyethylene film and scrap lumber. Dip plywood in water repellent or give thorough brush treatment. Double brush-coat all cut edges.
3. Assemble the seven frames. (See longitudinal section drawing.)
4. Select a well-drained site. Excavate hole deep enough so that shelter floor will be at least 2 feet below ground surface and wide enough to permit nailing of plywood sides to frames from outside. Slope bottom of the trench so that shelter will be 2 inches higher at entrance than at rear. Lay a 2-inch sandbed for polyethylene moisture barrier.

5. Place polyethylene moisture barrier in excavation and cover bottom with a 4-inch layer of sand to prevent frames from breaking barrier. (Sec. A–A, Front View.)

6. Cut three floor blocks to size and tack to underside of floor panel. Place the seven frames approximately in place, imbedded so that the sand will be flush with the underside of the floor panel. Then pass the floor panel inside the frames and nail in place.

7. Toe the end and side panels on the edges of floor panel and nail securely; then nail the side and top blocking, and finally, nail the top panel overlapping both the side and end panels.

8. Pad the outside top corners of the shelter to prevent damage to the polyethylene moisture barrier. Wrap the shelter with the polyethylene.

9. Backfill with 2 feet of earth cover after forming a sandbag retaining wall over the entrance (see longitudinal section) and alongside entranceway.

10. Provide enough filled sandbags or solid concrete blocks for a closure 2 feet thick in the entrance.

11. As an alternative to digging a large hole as described in step 4 above, a somewhat smaller hole can be used if the shelter is assembled above ground and lowered gently into the hole. The shelter weighs approximately 400 pounds complete, or 260 pounds without ends and top. Care must be taken to avoid puncturing the polyethylene moisture barrier.

12. If blower is installed, it should be supported by blocking, or by a frame attached to the end panel with 2″ x 4″ stiffeners.

NOTE: The size of the shelter may be increased in width and height. There is no arbitrary limit to length but the plywood sheets must butt each other at a frame. To increase the width from 4′ to 6′ use 2″ x 6″ ceiling joists. To increase the width from 6′ to 8′ use 2″ x 8″ ceiling joists. To increase the height from 4′ to 6′ use 2″ x 6″ wall studs and floor joists. When increasing height or width the ceiling joists should rest directly on the wall studs and be secured to them by means of nailed ⅜-inch plywood gussets. Ceiling joists require a gusset on one side only. Floor joists require a gusset on each side. Use 12 sixpenny nails in each gusset. Six nails should be used in each of the joined pieces.

BILL OF MATERIALS
(For 4′ x 8′ size)

Item	Quantity
⅜″ exterior plywood (Federal specification CS 45–60) or ½″ exterior plywood (Federal specification CS 122–60, group 1 or 2).	5 sheets.
2″ x 4″ x 10′ construction grade Douglas fir or equal	8 pieces.
2″ x 4″ x 8′ construction grade Douglas fir or equal	8 pieces.
4″ x 4′ plywood lumber (drip cap)	1 piece.
9 mil polyethylene film (16′ width)	20 feet.
Water repellent (5 percent pentachlorophenol or equal), toxic to wood-destroying fungi and insects.	2 gallons.
Eightpenny galvanized common nails	4 pounds.
Sixteenpenny galvanized common nails	3 pounds.
3″ diameter galvanized vent pipe	3½ feet.
Vent pipe cap	1.
3″ diameter 90° elbows	2.
Galvanized hinges	1 pair.
Flyscreen 7″ x 7″	1.
Sandbags	58.
Dry sand	3 tons.
Blower (optional, to be used with vent pipe, for 3-person size).	1.
Soil or sand (for shelter cover)	5 cubic yards.

Belowground Corrugated Steel Culvert Shelter

GENERAL INFORMATION

This shelter is designed to provide low-cost protection from the effects of radioactive fallout. Its principal advantages are that most of the structure is generally available as a prefabricated unit ready for lowering into an excavation and that it requires only simple connections and covering to complete the installation.

TECHNICAL SUMMARY

Space and Occupancy.—This shelter has 32 square feet of area and about 120 cubic feet of space (including the entranceway). It could provide space for three persons. The addition of a 4-foot length would provide for one more person.

Availability and Cost of Materials.—This type of shelter is available from steel culvert fabricators or their sales outlets in most population centers. This prefabricated shelter, including ventilation system, plastic wrap, and sandbags is designed to be sold for $150 or less, excluding delivery and installation.

Fallout Protection Factor.—When the entranceway is properly shielded as shown in the drawings, the protection factor should be greater than 500.

Blast Protection.—This shelter could be expected to withstand a limited blast overpressure of 5 pounds per square inch.

Ventilation.—A sheet metal intake vent 3 inches in diameter is provided together with a manual airblower for more than three persons. Air is vented through the sandbag closure at the entrance.

Installation Time.—One man working with hand excavation tools should be able to complete the excavation in less than 2 man-days. Two men will be needed to roll the shelter structure into the excavation from the point at which the shelter has been delivered. If lifting rather than rolling is necessary to transport the structure, four men will be required. Time for this phase will vary upward from 1 hour depending on distance of the move. It will then take one man 4 working days to complete the covering and installation phases.

Structural Life Expectancy.—The estimated life of this galvanized steel shelter will be at least 10 years under most soil conditions. Under normal conditions highway culverts of similar material have been known to last indefinitely with little maintenance.

CONSTRUCTION SEQUENCE*

1. Select well-drained site. The total area required, including the mounding, will be approximately 15' x 20'.
2. Use stakes to mark the corners of the area, and excavate. The hole required for the main shell is 5' x 9' x 2' deep, and the entrance requires an additional 2½' x 4' x 6''.
3. Line hole with plastic film wrap.
4. Lower galvanized steel shelter into place on supporting wood strips.
5. Assemble and install the vent pipe.
6. Cover shelter with plastic wrap.
7. Backfill and mound. Be sure the shelter is covered by at least 2 feet of packed earth. Depth may be checked with a wire probe. The mound should be covered with grass as soon as possible by sodding or seeding to prevent the protective soil from being eroded.
8. Place small sandbags inside the shelter. These are used to fill the entrance completely after the shelter is occupied.
9. 1-inch boards may be used on 2'' x 4'' blocks to provide a floor.

*This is a generalized construction sequence for a prefabricated steel culvert shelter. Detailed instructions are provided with the construction kit.

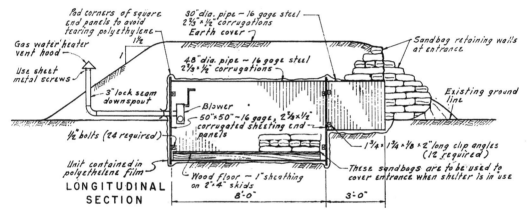

LONGITUDINAL SECTION

BILL OF MATERIALS
(To shelter 3 persons)

Item	Quantity
Prefabricated steel culvert shelter (with bolts and clips supplied, if unit is not spot welded).*	1.
Galvanized steel lock-seam downspout	6 feet.
Elbow for steel lock-seam downspout	1 foot.
Ventcap (gas water-heater type)	1.
Intake air blower (optional for 3 persons or less)	1.
Scrap lumber	9 board feet.
6 mil. polyethylene film (20' width)	30 feet.
Sandbags (to hold 75 to 100 pounds each)	18.
Sandbags (to hold 15 to 20 pounds each)	30.
Flyscreen 7'' x 7'', for ventpipe	1.
Entranceway insect screen 36'' x 36''	1.
Soil or sand (for shelter cover)	5 tons.

*Fabricators should treat spot-welded areas with bitumastic compound or other approved waterproofing material.

Outside Semimounded Steel Igloo Shelter

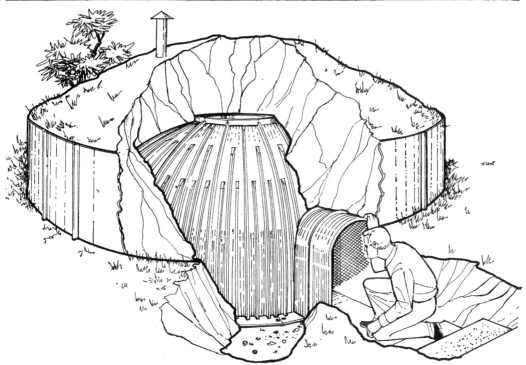

GENERAL INFORMATION

This shelter is designed to provide low-cost protection from the effects of radioactive fallout. Its principal advantages are that it provides fallout and limited blast protection and is suitable for either indoor or outdoor installation, and is easily assembled.

TECHNICAL SUMMARY

Space and Occupancy.—The shelter type detailed in this design has about 80 square feet of area including the entrance space. The interior has about 260 cubic feet and will house six persons.

Availability and Cost of Materials.—This shelter is of the prefabricated type and is available at department stores, building supply outlets, and mail-order firms. Cost is about $175, not including installation or delivery.

Fallout Protection Factor.—The protection factor should be about 500 with the prescribed thickness of covering and proper shielding of the entranceway.

Blast Protection.—This shelter could be expected to withstand a limited blast overpressure of 5 pounds per square inch.

Ventilation.—Ventilation is provided by a 3-inch intake pipe to which should be attached a hand operated blower. The air is vented through the airspace left in the entranceway.

Construction Time.—The igloo steel shell requires 4 man-hours to assemble. Excavating and covering time should take 24 man-hours.

Structural Life Expectancy.—The igloo, when coated with mastic, has a life expectancy of at least 10 years.

CONSTRUCTION SEQUENCE*

1. Select well-drained site. The total area required, including the mounding, will be approximately 15' x 20'.
2. Use stakes to mark the area, and excavate. The hole required for the main shell is 5' x 12' x 2' deep, and the entranceway requires an additional 2½' x 2' x 6''.
3. Line hole with plastic film wrap.
4. Bolt one wall panel to the roof crown.
5. Bolt the next wall panel to the roof crown 180° from the first wall panel.

6. The third wall panel should be bolted to the crown and to a mating section. Repeat this step until all panels are bolted to mating panels and to the roof crown.
7. To complete the shelter, bolt the crawl entrance to the flanged lip on the entrance panel.
8. Cut 3''-diameter hole in wall opposite entrance. Mount ventpipe.
9. For outdoor installations, mound sand, earth, or bags of sand over the igloo shell to a covering height of 2 feet.
10. As an alternate installation in a basement, mound loose sand or sandbags to a covering height of at least 18 inches over the igloo shell.

*This is a generalized construction sequence for a prefabricated igloo shelter. Detailed instructions are provided with the construction kit.

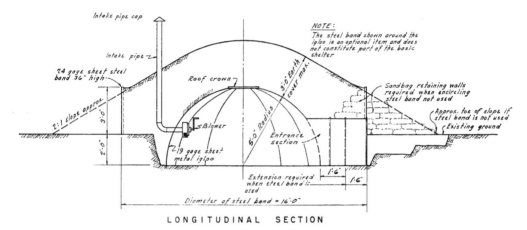

LONGITUDINAL SECTION

BILL OF MATERIALS

Item	Quantity
Roof crown	1.
Wall panels	11.
Wall panel, with entrance opening	1.
Entrance, crawlway and door	1.
Sand or soil for cover	15 tons.
6 mil. polyethylene film (20' wide)	30 feet.
Mastic	6 gallons
Ventpipe (3'' diameter) with ventpipe cap	6 feet.
Hand-operated blower (20 cubic feet per minute)	1.
Flyscreen 7'' x 7'' for ventpipe	1.
(Nuts, bolts, washers—as required.)	
Sandbags (to hold 15 to 20 pounds each) for entrance and retaining walls.	50.
Sandbags (to hold 75 to 100 pounds each)	30.

Aboveground Earth-Covered Lumber A-Frame Shelter

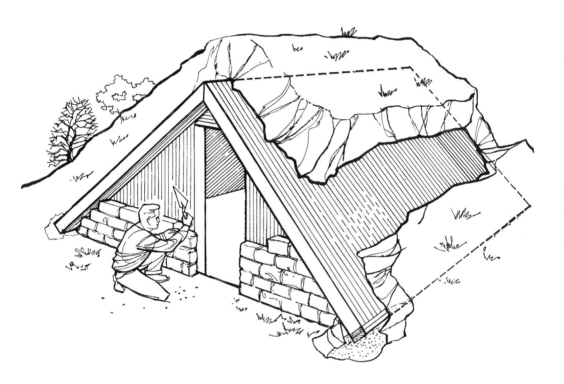

GENERAL INFORMATION

The purpose of this shelter is to provide protection for 10 persons from the effects of radioactive fallout at a location near but separate from a residence or other nearby buildings. The principal advantage of this shelter is that it can be erected without excavation in locations where there is poor drainage or where the ground water table is close to the surface. However, this shelter is not a low-cost structure. Footings or thrust ties are needed where the earth is soft or of poor bearing capacity.

TECHNICAL SUMMARY

Space and Occupancy.—This shelter provides almost 150 square feet of area and approximately 640 cubic feet of space. Although only a small portion of this area provides sufficient headroom for standing erect, practically the entire area can serve as sitdown space for 10 persons and storage space for supplies.

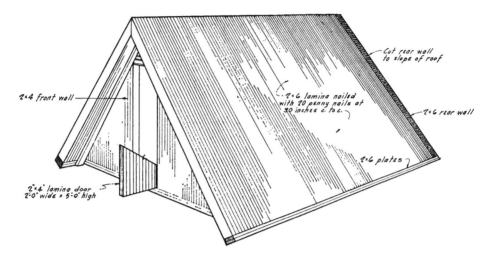

Cut rear wall to slope of roof

2×4 front wall

2×6 lamina nailed with 20 penny nails at 30 inches c. to c.

2×6 rear wall

2×6 plates

2×4 lamina door 2'-0" wide × 5'-0" high

PERSPECTIVE VIEW

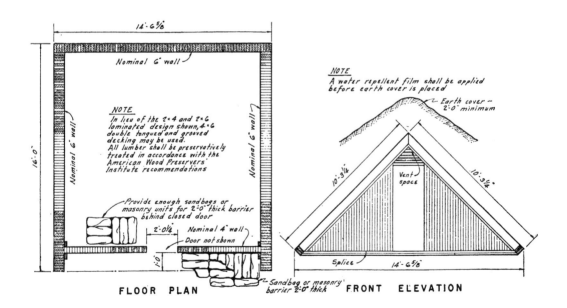

14'-6⅝"

Nominal 6" wall

Nominal 6" wall

Nominal 6" wall

16'-0"

NOTE
In lieu of the 2×4 and 2×6 laminated design shown, 4×6 double tongued and grooved decking may be used.
All lumber shall be preservatively treated in accordance with the American Wood Preservers' Institute recommendations

Provide enough sandbags or masonry units for 2'-0" thick barrier behind closed door

2'-0¼"

Nominal 4" wall

Door not shown

1'-0"

Sandbag or masonry barrier 2'-0" thick

FLOOR PLAN

NOTE
A water repellent film shall be applied before earth cover is placed

Earth cover — 2'-0" minimum

10'-3¼"

Vent space

10'-3¼"

Splice

14'-6⅝"

FRONT ELEVATION

70

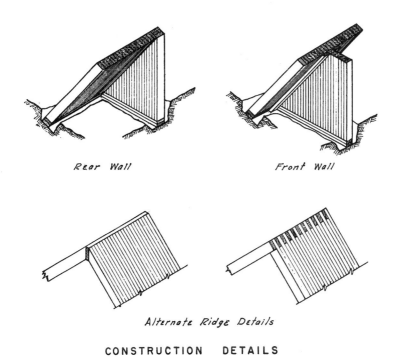

Rear Wall   *Front Wall*

Alternate Ridge Details

CONSTRUCTION DETAILS

Availability and Cost of Materials.—The pressure-treated lumber which is required is generally available at retail lumberyards. In certain areas it may be necessary to allow time for the treated lumber to be ordered and transported from stock at other locations. The estimated cost of materials is $550.

Fallout Protection Factor.—The recommended minimum earth cover of 2 feet with an entranceway and door shielded by a 2-foot thickness of sandbags, and the rear wall mounded will provide a protection factor of about 500.

Blast Protection.—While the basic function of this shelter is fallout protection, limited blast resistance of about 5 pounds per square inch of overpressure would be afforded by the heavy wood structure. The blast resistance would vary somewhat with the workmanship and materials but the laminated design tends to offset variations.

Ventilation.—Ducts for mechanical ventilation may be located in the ventspace over the doorway without involving structural change. Hand-operated ventilation equipment should be used.

Construction Time.—After materials are delivered at the jobsite, 4 man-days should be allowed for erecting the structure. Earth covering would require 4 additional man-days, without the use of power equipment.

Structural Life Expectancy.—The life expectancy of this shelter should be from 15 to 20 years.

CONSTRUCTION SEQUENCE

1. Assemble the materials at the shelter site.
2. Trench to subsoil for the wallplates as shown on the floor plan and details. Assemble plates in the trenches. (See construction details, rear-front walls.)
3. Begin at either end and erect roof wall members in pairs. (See alternate ridge details.) Progress to the opposite end, spiking laminations together. If 2" x 6" lamina are used, they should be nailed with twentypenny nails at approximately 30-inch spacing. If 4" x 6" decking lamina are used, they should be fastened together with 5/16-inch diameter spikes at approximately 30-inch spacing.
4. Erect the end walls as shown on the drawings with ends of the lamina cut flush with the roof wall top surface. The lamina should be spiked together in the same manner as the roof members.
5. The supporting structure is now complete. It should be covered with the polyethylene film and covered with earth. The earth cover should be started at the base of the roof walls and applied evenly to both sides. Next mound earth against the rear wall. The sandbags or masonry blocks are applied on both sides of the front wall to a thickness of 2 feet. A supply of filled sandbags or blocks should be stored inside the shelter to add to the protection afforded by the door.
6. Vegetation, riprap, or other means of holding the soil in place should be provided.
7. A duct for air intake will be required with the installation of the hand-operated blower. The intake duct may be located in the rear wall of the shelter and the air can be exhausted through the louvered ventspace over the doorway.
8. The door may be of heat- or blast-resistant construction, as manufactured commercially, or may be contrived by nailing 2" x 4" studs together to make a 4-inch-thick door. This then can be mounted with ordinary hinges and should be painted white.

BILL OF MATERIALS

Item	Quantity
Roof walls 2" x 6" x 10'	250 pieces.
Rear wall 2" x 6" x 8'	50 pieces.
Front wall 2" x 4" x 8'	40 pieces.
Plates:	
2" x 6" x 10'	10 pieces.
2" x 4" x 10'	3 pieces.
Fastenings:	
Fortypenny nails	10 pounds.
Twentypenny nails	30 pounds.
Water repellent—building felt or plastic film	150 square feet.
Bagged earth or masonry blocks for front wall shielding.	600 filled sandbags (30 pounds) or 176 concrete blocks (8" x 12" x 16").
Blower, manually operated (rated at 30 cubic feet per minute).	1.
Intake pipe, galvanized (to be mounted through rear wall).	6 feet.
Flyscreen 7" x 7" (for intake pipe)	1.
Flyscreen 24" x 24" (to cover ventspace over door)	1.

Belowground New Construction Clay Masonry Shelter

GENERAL INFORMATION

This shelter will provide protection against the effects of radioactive fallout. It can also protect from limited blast overpressures. The shelter is located belowground outside a house but is reached from the basement. Its principal advantages are in flexibility of shape and design to conform to the house design and in the use of materials that tie in with the new construction of a house. Because of the headroom and interior space the shelter can be used for other purposes.

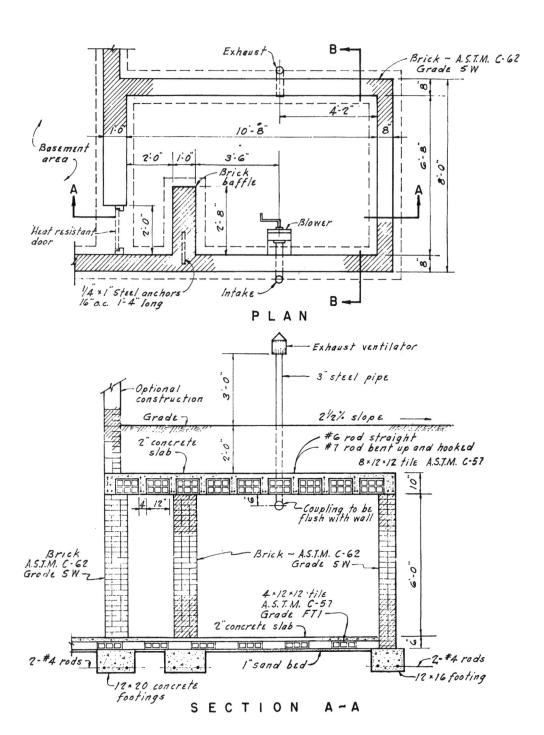

PLAN

SECTION A-A

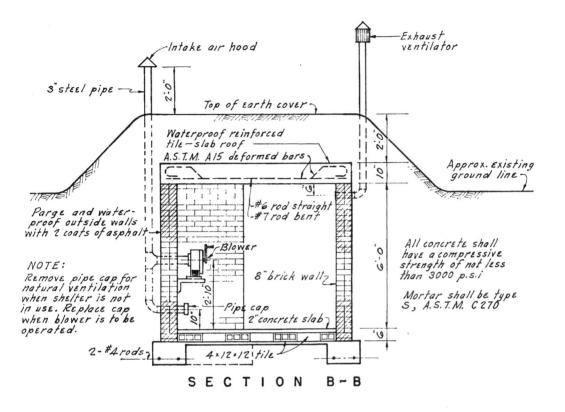

SECTION B-B

Labels in figure:
- Intake air hood
- Exhaust ventilator
- 3" steel pipe
- 2'-0"
- Top of earth cover
- Waterproof reinforced tile—slab roof
- A.S.T.M. A15 deformed bars
- 2'-0"
- 10'
- Approx. existing ground line
- Parge and waterproof outside walls with 2 coats of asphalt
- #6 rod straight
- #7 rod bent
- Blower
- 8" brick wall
- All concrete shall have a compressive strength of not less than 3000 p.s.i
- Mortar shall be type S, A.S.T.M. C270
- 6'-0"
- NOTE: Remove pipe cap for natural ventilation when shelter is not in use. Replace cap when blower is to be operated.
- 2'-10"
- 10"
- Pipe cap
- 2" concrete slab
- 6"
- 2-#4 rods
- 4×12×12 tile

TECHNICAL SUMMARY

Space and Occupancy.—The shelter in this design has over 70 square feet of area and 420 cubic feet of space. It will provide occupancy for six persons.

Availability and Cost of Materials.—Structural clay masonry units, brick, and structural tile are available at your local building materials supplier. Cost of the materials and equipment for the basic shelter is estimated at $300 to $350. Labor cost should run approximately $250 to $300 when performed as part of new house construction.

Fallout Protection Factor.—The protection factor for a shelter of this type is over 1000.

Blast Protection.—This shelter has a structural blast resistance of 5-pounds-per-square-inch overpressure.

Ventilation.—Ventilation equipment and pipe are required. A hand-operated blower should be specified to furnish at least 20 cubic feet of air per minute. The air is exhausted through a separate ventpipe.

Construction Time.—A home-construction project that includes this shelter will not require additional trades or crafts not already on the project. The time for construction of this shelter could increase normal house construction time by a few days.

Structural Life Expectancy.—Assuming normal construction practices, this structure, with a minimum of maintenance, should last more than 30 years.

CONSTRUCTION SEQUENCE

No construction sequence is given for this shelter because the work would probably be supervised by a contractor familiar with new construction.

BILL OF MATERIALS

Item	Quantity
Roof:	
8″ x 12″ x 12″ structural clay tile ASTM–C57—grade FTI.	72 pieces.
Steel reinforcing, No. 6 deformed bars 7′6″ length, ASTM–A–15—Straight.	10 pieces.
Steel reinforcing, No. 7 deformed bars 10′ length, bent up and hooked ASTM–A–15.	10 pieces.
Concrete, minimum 3,000 pounds per square inch	1.5 cubic yards.
Walls:	
Brick, standard size (2⅔″ x 4″ x 8″) ASTM–C62—grade SW.	3,800 pieces.
Anchors (¼″ x 1″ x 4″) steel	4.
Mortar (1–¼–3¾ cement-lime-sand)	65 cubic feet.
Floor:	
Tile (4″ x 12″ x 12″) structural clay ASTM–C57—grade FTI.	96 pieces.
Concrete, minimum 3,000 pounds per square inch	0.7 cubic yard.
Footings:	
Concrete, minimum 3,000 pounds per square inch	1.0 cubic yard.
Steel reinforcing, No. 4 reinforcing bars ASTM–A15	68 linear feet.
Miscellaneous:	
Parge 1–¼–3¾ mortar ASTM–C270—Type M	8 cubic feet.
Asphalt	5 gallons.
Blower (at least 20-cubic-feet-per-minute rating)	1.
Mounting bracket, blower	1.
Intake and exhaust ventpipe, 3″ steel (sufficient for both intake and vent pipes).	16 linear feet.
Fittings:	
Ells 3″ steel	2.
Tees 3″ steel	1.
Ventpipe cap	1.
Flyscreen 7″ x 7″ (for vent and intake pipes)	2.

U.S. GOVERNMENT PRINTING OFFICE: 1962

You
Can
SURVIVE

Executive Office of the President
National Security Resources Board
Civil Defense Office
NSRB Doc. 130

You can live through an atom bomb raid

and you won't have to have a Geiger counter

protective clothing, or special training

in order to do it.

The secrets of survival are:

KNOW THE BOMB'S TRUE DANGERS.

KNOW THE STEPS YOU CAN TAKE
TO ESCAPE THEM.

To begin with, you must realize that atom-splitting is just another way of causing an explosion. While an atom bomb holds more death and destruction than man has ever before wrapped in a single package, its total power is definitely limited. Not even hydrogen bombs could blow the earth apart or kill us all by mysterious radiation.

**YOUR CHANCES
OF SURVIVING
AN ATOMIC ATTACK
ARE BETTER THAN
YOU MIGHT HAVE
THOUGHT.**

Because the power of all bombs is limited, your chances of living through an atomic attack are much better than you may have thought. In the city of Hiroshima, slightly over half the people who were a mile from the atomic explosion are still alive. At Nagasaki, almost 70 percent of the people a mile from the bomb lived to tell their experiences. Today thousands of survivors of these two atomic attacks live in new houses built right where their old ones once stood. The war may have changed their way of life, but they are not riddled with cancer. Their children are normal. Those who were temporarily unable to have children because of the radiation now are having children again.

WHAT ARE YOUR CHANCES?

If a modern A-bomb exploded without warning in the air over your home town tonight, your calculated chances of living through the raid would run something like this:

Should you happen to be one of the unlucky people right under the bomb, there is practically

"Modern" atomic bomb, as used in this booklet, refers to the "nominal" bomb described in the "Effects of Atomic Weapons," published in June 1950 by the Atomic Energy Commission.

no hope of living through it. In fact, anywhere within one-half mile of the center of explosion, your chances of escaping are about 1 out of 10.

On the other hand, and this is the important point, from one-half to 1 mile away, you have a 50-50 chance.

From 1 to 1½ miles out, the odds that you will be killed are only 15 in 100.

And at points from 1½ to 2 miles away, deaths drop all the way down to only 2 or 3 out of each 100.

Beyond 2 miles, the explosion will cause practically no deaths at all.

Naturally, your chances of being injured are far greater than your chances of being killed. But even injury by radioactivity does not mean that you will be left a cripple, or doomed to die an early death. Your chances of making a complete recovery are much the same as for everyday accidents. These estimates hold good for modern atomic bombs exploded without warning.

WHAT ABOUT SUPER BOMBS?

Do not be misled by loose talk of imaginary weapons a hundred or a thousand times as powerful. All cause destruction by exactly the same means, yet one 20,000-ton bomb would not create nearly as much damage as 10,000 two-ton bombs dropped a little distance apart. This is because the larger bombs "waste" too much power near the center of the explosion. From the practical point of view, it doesn't matter whether a build-

BEYOND A HALF MILE, YOUR CHANCES OF SURVIVING INCREASE RAPIDLY.

INJURY BY RADIOACTIVITY DOES NOT NECESSARILY MEAN YOU ARE DOOMED TO DIE OR BE CRIPPLED.

DON'T BE MISLED BY WILD TALK OF 'SUPER-SUPER BOMBS'.

ing near the center of the explosion is completely vaporized or whether it is simply knocked into a pile of rubble.

To be more specific, a modern atomic bomb can do heavy damage to houses and buildings roughly 2 miles away. But doubling its power will extend the range of damage to only about 2½ miles. In the same way, if there were a bomb 100 times as powerful, it would reach out only a little more than 4½, not 100 times as far.

And remember: All these calculations of your chances of survival assume that you have absolutely **no** advance warning of the attack.

Just like fire bombs and ordinary high explosives, atomic weapons cause most of their death and damage by blast and heat. So first let's look at a few things you can do to escape these two dangers.

WHAT ABOUT BLAST?

Even if you have only a second's warning, there is one important thing you can do to lessen your chances of injury by blast: Fall flat on your face.

More than half of all wounds are the result of being bodily tossed about or being struck by falling and flying objects. If you lie down flat, you are least likely to be thrown about. If you have time to pick a good spot, there is less chance of your being struck by flying glass and other things.

If you are inside a building, the best place to flatten out is close against the cellar wall. If you haven't time to get down there, lie down along an inside wall, or duck under a bed or table. But don't pick a spot right opposite the windows or you are almost sure to be pelted with shattered glass.

If caught out-of-doors, either drop down alongside the base of a good substantial building—avoid flimsy, wooden ones likely to be blown over on top of you—or else jump in any handy ditch or gutter.

When you fall flat to protect yourself from a bombing, don't look up to see what is coming. Even during the daylight hours, the flash from a bursting A-bomb can cause several moments of blindness, if you're facing that way. To prevent it, bury your face in your arms and hold it there for 10 or 12 seconds after the explosion. That will also help to keep flying glass and other things out of your eyes.

WHAT ABOUT BURNS?

Flash burns from the A-bomb's light and heat caused about 30 percent of the injuries at Hiroshima and Nagasaki. Near the center of the burst the burns are often fatal. People may be seriously burned more than a mile away, while the heat can be felt on the bare face and hands at 4 or 5 miles.

To prevent flash burns, try to find a shelter where there is a wall, a high bank or some other object between you and the bursting bomb. You can expect that the bomber will aim for the city's biggest collection of industrial buildings.

A little bit of solid material will provide flash

IN YOUR HOUSE: LIE DOWN AGAINST A WALL.

OUTDOORS: GET NEXT TO A SOLID BUILDING.

TO ESCAPE TEMPORARY BLINDNESS, BURY YOUR FACE IN YOUR ARMS.

FLASH BURNS ARE A SERIOUS CAUSE OF INJURY. SHIELD YOURSELF FROM THE FLASH.

protection even close to the explosion. Farther out, the thinnest sort of thing—even cotton cloth—will often do the trick.

If you work in the open, always wear full-length, loose-fitting, light-colored clothes in time of emergency. Never go around with your sleeves rolled up. Always wear a hat—the brim may save you a serious face burn.

EVEN A LITTLE MATERIAL GIVES PROTECTION FROM FLASH BURNS, SO BE SURE TO DRESS PROPERLY.

WHAT ABOUT RADIOACTIVITY?

In all stories about atomic weapons, there is a great deal about radioactivity.

Radioactivity is the only way—besides size—in which the effects of A or H bombs are different from ordinary bombs. But, with the exception of underwater or ground explosions, the radioactivity from atomic bursts is much less to be feared than blast and heat.

RADIOACTIVITY IS THE ONLY WAY BESIDES SIZE IN WHICH ATOMIC BOMBS DIFFER FROM ORDINARY ONES.

Radioactivity is not new or mysterious. In the form of cosmic rays from the sky, all of us have been continually bombarded by radiation every hour and day of our lives. We all have also breathed and eaten very small amounts of radioactive materials without even knowing it. For over half a century, doctors and scientists have experimented and worked with X-rays and other penetrating forms of energy. Because of all this experience, we actually know much more about radioactivity and what it does to people than we know about infantile paralysis, colds, or some other common diseases.

WE KNOW MORE ABOUT RADIOACTIVITY THAN WE DO ABOUT CLOUDS

It is easy to understand how radioactivity works if we think of how sunlight behaves.

In the northern part of the world, winter's slanting sun rays seldom cause sunburn, but the hotter rays of the summer sun often do. Still, just a few moments in the midsummer sun will not give you a tan or sunburn. You have to stay in its hot rays for some time before you get a burn. What's more, bad sunburn on just the face and hands may hurt, but it won't seriously harm you. On the other hand, if it covers your whole body, it can make you very sick, or sometimes even cause death.

In the same way, the harm that can come to you from radioactivity will depend on the power of the rays and particles that strike you, upon the length of time you are exposed to them, and on how much of your body is exposed.

INJURY FROM RADIOACTOVITY DEPENDS ON THE POWER OF THE RAYS AND PARTICLES, HOW LONG YOU ARE EXPOSED AND HOW MUCH YOUR BODY WAS HIT.

WHAT IS "INITIAL" RADIOACTIVITY?

Broadly speaking, atomic explosions produce two different kinds of radioactivity. First—and most important in an air burst—is an extremely powerful invisible burst of rays and particles thrown off at the time of explosion. This kind is called "initial" or explosive radioactivity. Its rays and particles fly out quickly, then promptly die. There is danger from them only for little more than a minute. The second type of radioactivity—lingering radioactivity—will be described later.

EXPLOSIVE RADIOACTIVITY IS THE MOST IMPORTANT KIND, BUT IT LASTS ONLY A MOMENT.

The injury range of the explosive radioactivity from a modern A-bomb is a little over 1 mile, if the bomb is exploded about 2,000 feet in the air. If it is exploded much higher, some of the radiation may not reach the ground, so the range may be less. If it is exploded much lower, the radiation also may not reach out as far, because it would be blocked by the ground or by buildings.

A little more than a mile away, the principal effects of the few dying rays that struck you could be seen only as temporary blood changes in a doctor's examination. You probably wouldn't even realize you had been exposed.

A little less than a mile from the explosion center, if you are unprotected, you are almost sure to suffer illness. Less than two-thirds of a mile away, those caught in the open are pretty sure to soak up a fatal dose of radioactivity.

Still, the possibility of your being caught without some protection is not very great. Even if you are on the street, there is a good chance that a building, or many buildings, will be between you and the burst, and they will partially or completely shield you.

Atomic explosions high above ground cause the most widespread damage. And, as happened in Japan, when an A-bomb goes off in the air you are far more likely to be hurt by the bomb's blast and heat waves than by its radioactivity. At Hiroshima and Nagasaki slightly over one-half of all deaths and injuries were caused by blast. Nearly one-third of the casualties were from the heat flash.

THE BIGGEST DANGER FROM EXPLOSIVE RADIOACTIVITY LIES WITHIN A MILE OF THE EXPLOSION.

BUILDINGS WILL PARTIALLY OR COMPLETELY SHIELD YOU.

YOU ARE MORE LIKELY TO BE HURT BY BLAST AND HEAT THAN BY RADIATION.

Radioactivity alone caused only about 15 percent of all deaths and injuries

If the bomb were to go off close to the ground, or slightly below its surface, the range of the explosive radiation, as well as the range of the blast and heat, would be reduced. This is due to the fact that all three would be partially blocked by the earth, by nearby buildings and by other obstacles.

In an underwater burst, there would be much less to fear from blast and nothing to fear from heat. Practically all the explosive radioactivity would be absorbed by the water. However, there would be the second type of radioactivity to be described later on.

EXPLOSIVE RADIOACTIVITY IS LESS OF A DANGER IN GROUND-LEVEL OR UNDERWATER BURSTS.

WHAT ABOUT "INDUCED" RADIOACTIVITY?

If an atomic bomb goes off in the air within two-thirds of a mile or slightly more of your home, there is no practical way of keeping explosive radioactivity out of the above-ground part of your house. It is possible that, at very short range, artificial, or induced radioactivity could be set up in gold, silver, and many other objects. However, this kind of radioactivity will never offer great danger, so don't throw away bandages and other first aid materials in the medicine cabinet. They will be perfectly safe to use.

EXPLOSIVE RADIOACTIVITY CAN'T BE KEPT OUT OF UPPER FLOORS OF YOUR HOUSE, SO LEARN WHAT TO EXPECT FROM IT.

85

EVEN CANNED
AND BOTTLED
FOODS MAY BE
RADIATED, BUT
IT WILL STILL BE
SAFE TO USE THEM.

Naturally, the radioactivity that passes through the walls of your house won't be stopped by tin or glass. It can go right through canned and bottled foods. However, this will not make them dangerous, and it will not cause them to spoil. Go ahead and use them, provided the containers are not broken open.

WHAT ABOUT "RADIATION SICKNESS"?

VOMITING AND
DIARRHEA ARE
THE FIRST SIGNS
OF RADIATION
SICKNESS.

Should you be caught upstairs or in the open at the time of a bombing, you might soak up a serious dose of explosive radioactivity. Even so, the first indication that you had been pierced by the rays probably wouldn't show up for a couple of hours. Then you most likely would get sick at your stomach and begin to vomit. However, you might be sick at your stomach for other reasons, too, so vomiting won't always mean you have radiation sickness. The time it would take you to get sick would depend on how strong a dose you got. The stronger the dose, the quicker you would get sick. For a few days you might continue to feel below par and about 2 weeks later most of your hair might fall out. By the time you lost your hair you would be good and sick. But in spite of it all, you would still stand better than an even chance of making a complete recovery, including having your hair grow in again.

EVEN IF YOU
SHOULD GET
SEVERE RADIATION
SICKNESS, YOU
WOULD HAVE BETTER
THAN AN EVEN
CHANCE OF
RECOVERY.

WHERE IS THE BEST PLACE TO GO?

If your house is close to the explosion, there is little you can do to protect it from the bomb's blast, or pressure wave. Within one-half mile of the surface point directly beneath the explosion, the shock wave from an atomic bomb is sure to flatten most houses. Out to a distance of about 1 mile, steel, brick, and wooden structures are likely to be damaged beyond repair. Farther out, there is less destruction, but serious damage may be expected to extend as far as 2 miles.

It is only wise to figure that the upper floors of most buildings near the explosion will be pushed in. This means the basement is probably the safest place to be. If you have a basement and time to get down to it, lie flat along the outer wall or near the base of some heavy supporting column. You would be even safer under a cellar work bench or heavy table. Stay away from the middle of the floor where falling beams and other objects are most likely to strike you.

Naturally, you run a risk of being trapped in the wreckage, but your *over-all* chances of escape from the bomb in most cases are many times greater than they would be upstairs. If your basement has two exits, you will be in less danger of being trapped.

Besides protecting you from blast and heat, basements also provide shielding from explosive radia-

87

BASEMENTS GIVE SHELTER AGAINST BLAST AND HEAT, AND RADIOACTIVITY.

tion. Because, the lower you get, the more barriers against radiation there are likely to be between you and the bursting bomb. Down in the cellar you'll probably be shielded not only by other buildings, but also by earth and the cement foundations of your own house. Earth, concrete and steel are good radiation barriers.

IF YOU HAVE NO BASEMENT, LOCATE A SHELTER YOU CAN REACH QUICKLY.

If you have no basement, look around your immediate neighborhood for a nearby shelter you can get to quickly in an emergency. Such a shelter might be a culvert, a deep gully, or another building within easy reach. If you live in rolling country, there is probably a hill close to you. Even a high bank will offer some protection from most bursts if it is between you and the explosion. In choosing your shelter, assume that the enemy will aim for the industrial buildings.

CYCLONE CELLARS ARE EXCELLENT.

If you live in a State where there is danger from sudden storms like cyclones or hurricanes, you may have a "cyclone cellar" or something similar. If so, you have a shelter that will give excellent protection against atomic bombs.

HOW SHOULD A HOUSE BE PREPARED?

"FIREPROOF HOUSEKEEPING" IS IMPORTANT.

Starting right now you should go in for "fireproof housekeeping." Don't let trash pile up around your house and always keep it in covered containers.

KILL THE MYTHS

ATOMIC WEAPONS WILL NOT DESTROY THE EARTH

Atomic bombs hold .more death and destruction than man ever before has wrapped up in a single package, but their over-all power still has very definite limits. Not even hydrogen bombs will blow the earth apart or kill us all by radioactivity.

DOUBLING BOMB POWER DOES NOT DOUBLE DESTRUCTION

Modern A-bombs can cause heavy damage 2 miles away, but doubling their power would extend that range only to 2½ miles. To stretch the damage range from 2 to 4 miles would require a weapon more than *8 times* the rated power of present models.

RADIOACTIVITY IS NOT THE BOMB'S GREATEST THREAT

In most atom raids, blast and heat are by far the greatest dangers that people must face. Radioactivity alone would account for only a small percentage of all human deaths and injuries, except in underground or underwater explosions.

RADIATION SICKNESS IS NOT ALWAYS FATAL

In small amounts, radioactivity seldom is harmful. Even when serious radiation sickness follows a heavy dosage, there is still a good chance for recovery.

<u>ALWAYS</u> PUT FIRST THINGS FIRST AND

1. TRY TO GET SHIELDED

If you have time, get down in a basement or subway. Should you unexpectedly be caught out-of-doors, seek shelter alongside a building, or jump in any handy ditch or gutter.

2. DROP FLAT ON GROUND OR FLOOR

To keep from being tossed about and to lessen the chances of being struck by falling and flying objects, flatten out at the base of a wall, or at the bottom of a bank.

3. BURY YOUR FACE IN YOUR ARMS

When you drop flat, hide your eyes in the crook of your elbow. That will protect your face from flash burns, prevent temporary blindness and keep flying objects out of your eyes.

FOR ATOMIC ATTACKS

NEVER LOSE YOUR HEAD AND

4. DON'T RUSH OUTSIDE RIGHT AFTER A BOMBING

After an air burst, wait a few minutes
then go help to fight fires. After other kinds
of bursts wait at least 1 hour to give lingering
radiation some chance to die down.

5. DON'T TAKE CHANCES WITH FOOD OR WATER IN OPEN CONTAINERS

To prevent radioactive poisoning or
disease, select your food and water with
care. When there is reason to believe
they may be contaminated, stick to canned
and bottled things if possible.

6. DON'T START RUMORS

In the confusion that follows a bombing, a
single rumor might touch off a panic that
could cost your life.

FIVE KEYS TO HOUSEHOLD SAFETY

1. STRIVE FOR "FIREPROOF HOUSEKEEPING"

Don't let trash pile up, and keep waste paper in covered containers. When an alert sounds, do all you can to eliminate sparks by shutting off the oil burner and covering all open flames.

2. KNOW YOUR OWN HOME

Know which is the safest part of your cellar, learn how to turn off your oil burner and what to do about utilities.

3. HAVE EMERGENCY EQUIPMENT AND SUPPLIES HANDY

Always have a good flashlight, a radio, first-aid equipment and a supply of canned goods in the house.

4. CLOSE ALL WINDOWS AND DOORS AND DRAW THE BLINDS

If you have time when an alert sounds, close the house up tight in order to keep out fire sparks and radioactive dusts and to lessen the chances of being cut by flying glass. Keep the house closed until all danger is past.

5. USE THE TELEPHONE ONLY FOR TRUE EMERGENCIES

Do not use the phone unless absolutely necessary. Leave the lines open for real emergency traffic.

If you know you have time when an alert sounds, be sure to shut the doors and windows and pull down the shades. This will help keep out fire sparks.

If you have shutters or venetian blinds, or heavy drapes, they will also provide some protection against harm from flying glass.

Several other household precautions should be taken promptly. Atomic bombs set off high above ground seldom cause breaks in underground gas or water mains. However, shaking and twisting of the buildings by the blast wave sometimes snaps off household inlets at the point where they enter the basement. This may allow gas or oil to flow into your cellar.

To lessen the danger of fires and explosions that could result from this leakage, you should throw the electric switch that shuts off your oil burner.

Your local utility companies can give you detailed instructions about your gas, pilot lights, and so on.

If you have a coal-burning furnace or wood stove, be sure to close all its fuel and draft doors. In other words, do all you can to prevent sparks and to put out or cover open flames.

Should attack come without warning, take these same precautions right after the raid. Keep at least one flashlight handy and don't strike a match to light your way down into a darkened basement. Gas or oil fumes may be present and an explosion could result.

WHEN ALERTED, CLOSE ALL WINDOWS AND DOORS AND GUARD AGAINST INJURY BY FLYING GLASS.

TO PREVENT HOUSEHOLD EXPLOSIONS, SHUT OFF OIL BURNERS.

LOCAL UTILITY COMPANIES WILL GIVE YOU DETAILED INSTRUCTIONS ABOUT GAS, ELECTRICITY AND SO ON.

KEEP A FLASH-LIGHT HANDY.

WHAT ABOUT LINGERING RADIOACTIVITY?

Knowing how to protect yourself from blast, heat, and explosive radioactivity, only one major problem remains: That is how to avoid harm from lingering radioactivity.

Explosive radioactivity bursts from the bomb at the time of explosion and lasts for only little more than a minute.

Lingering radioactivity remains for a longer time, from a few minutes to weeks or months, depending on the kind of radioactive material.

Lingering radioactivity may become a danger when atomic bombs are exploded on the ground, underground, or in the water. Air bursts leave no dangerous lingering radioactivity.

Most lingering radioactivity comes from left-over bomb wastes, or "ashes," technically called fission products. They consist of countless billions of fragments, or pieces, of atoms split up in the explosion. Smaller, and usually less dangerous, amounts of lingering radioactivity may be thrown off by scattered atoms of uranium or plutonium that fail to split up when the bomb goes off.

These totally invisible radioactive particles act much the same as ordinary, everyday dust. When present in any real quantity, they are scattered about in patches and contaminate, or pollute, everything they fall on, including people. While they can be removed easily from some surfaces, they stick very tightly to others. It is practically impossible to get absolutely all of them out of household corners and cracks. Most of the time, it is far easier to prevent pollution than it is to remove it.

WHAT ABOUT RADIOACTIVE CLOUDS?

In spite of the huge quantities of lingering radioactivity loosed by atomic explosions, people fortunately are not very likely to be exposed to dangerous amounts of it in most atomic raids.

Since high-level bursts do the greatest damage, that is the kind we can expect most often. When atomic weapons are exploded in mid-air, the violent, upward surge of super-hot gases and air quickly sweeps practically all the radioactive ashes and unexploded bits of bomb fuel high into the sky. Most of them are carried harmlessly off in the drifting bomb clouds. High-level explosions definitely will not create "areas of doom", where no man dares enter and no plant can grow. In fact, they will leave very little radioactivity on the ground, even near the point of explosion. Fire-fighters and rescue teams can move promptly toward the center of destruction with little danger of facing harmful radiation.

IN AIR BURSTS RADIOACTIVE DUSTS ARE SPREAD SO WIDELY THAT THEY ARE UNLIKELY TO HARM PEOPLE.

AIR BURSTS WILL NOT CREATE 'AREAS OF DOOM'.

DON'T WORRY ABOUT HIGH-LEVEL RADIOACTIVITY.

Flash test dummies
A mother mannequin and her child doll take shelter in a basement just before an Operation Doorstep nuclear test in 1953. *(US Department of Energy)* Instructions for building this type of Lumber Lean-To Shelter are given on pages 49–50.

Right: The less than encouraging cover for *Survival Under Atomic Attack*. It was published in 1950 by the US Government Printing Office. An excerpt from this publication begins on page 77.